the MAINE FARM TABLE COOKBOOK

the MAINE FARM TABLE COOKBOOK

125 Homegrown Recipes
from the Pine Tree State

KATE SHAFFER

with photography by
DEREK BISSONNETTE

The Countryman Press
A Division of W. W. Norton & Company
Independent Publishers Since 1923

For information about permission to reproduce selections
  from this book, write to Permissions, The Countryman
  Press, 500 Fifth Avenue, New York, NY 10110

For information about special discounts for bulk purchases,
  please contact W. W. Norton Special Sales at
  specialsales@wwnorton.com or 800-233-4830

Manufacturing by Versa Press
Art director: Allison Chi
Production manager: Devon Zahn

Library of Congress Cataloging-in-Publication Data

Names: Shaffer, Kate, author.
Title: The Maine farm table cookbook : 125 homegrown
  recipes from the Pine Tree State / Kate Shaffer.
Description: New York, NY : The Countryman Press, a
  division of W. W. Norton & Company, Independent
  Publishers Since 1923, [2021] | Includes index.
Identifiers: LCCN 2020048980 | ISBN 9781682684856
  (pbk.) | ISBN 9781682684863 (epub)
Subjects: LCSH: Cooking, American—New England style. |
  Cooking—Maine. | Cooking (Fish) | Cooking (Lobsters) |
  LCGFT: Cookbooks.
Classification: LCC TX715.2.N48 S52 2021 | DDC
  641.5974—dc23
LC record available at https://lccn.loc.gov/2020048980

The Countryman Press
www.countrymanpress.com

A division of W. W. Norton & Company, Inc.
500 Fifth Avenue, New York, NY 10110
www.wwnorton.com

978-1-68268-485-6 (pbk.)

10 9 8 7 6 5 4 3 2 1

Recipe Credits:

Maine Grains Maple Granola (page 20): The Miller's Table at
  Maine Grains
Ployes (page 24): Janice Bouchard
Tortillería Pachanga Chorizo Molotes (page 38): Lynne Rowe
Tinder Hearth's Sourdough Whole Spelt Bread (page 44):
  Lydia Moffet
Beth Schiller's Wilted Frisée Salad with Ground Lamb and
  Fresh Chile (page 54): Beth Schiller
Schooner *Stephen Taber*'s Stuffed Fried Squash Blossoms
  (page 58): Noah Barnes
Erin French's Fried Green Tomatoes with Buttermilk & Chives
  (page 64) and Erin French's Spring Bread Salad with
  Asparagus, Radishes, Peas & Mint (page 67): Reprinted
  from *The Lost Kitchen* © 2017 by Erin French
Sara Jenkins's Eggplant Parmesan (page 94): Sara Jenkins
Meg Mitchell's Sweet Onion Pie (page 101): Margaret
  Mitchell
Blue Hill Blondes Oven-Baked Short Ribs (page 120): Betty
  Tyler
Aragosta's Blue Hill Bay Mussels with Crispy Kale (page
  149): Devin Finigan
Oysters on the Half Shell with Shallot Mignonette (page
  154): Abigail Carroll
Luke's Lobster Rolls (page 172): Benjamin Conniff
El El Frijoles Lobster Tacos (page 174), Spiced Achiote
  Butter (page 212), and Red Onion and Jalapeño Quick
  Pickle (page 288): Michele Levesque
Lobster Carbonara (page 178): Linda Greenlaw
UNION's Pan-Seared Local Hake with Littleneck Clams,
  Bok Choy, Chinese-Fermented Sausage, and Soy Brown
  Butter (page 185): Joshua Berry
Moose Bourguignon (page 194): Ken Burkett
Home-"Churned" Butter (page 212): Katia Holmes
Honey Butter Popcorn (page 214): Jennell Carter & Alicia
  Menard
Snell Farm Apple Pie (page 234): Abby Snell
Two Fat Cats Lemon Zucchini Whoopie Pies with Blueberry
  Filling (page 254): Stacy Begin
Wild Fern Apple-Cranberry Pie (page 267): Sarah Havener
  Brown

This book is dedicated to my husband, Steve, who has the weirdest ideas.

Twenty-one years ago he said, "In Maine, we can do anything. Let's go."

CONTENTS

ACKNOWLEDGMENTS

There are over 7,500 operating farms in Maine. That represents thousands more people who work to put fresh, close-to-home food on our plates every single day. I wish I could have written about them all. The same is true for the intensely creative chefs and innovative food producers using ingredients produced by friends and neighbors, connecting us all to this dynamic, essential, life-giving system. I wish I could have told all their stories.

But there are only so many pages in this book, and the unglamorous truth is that writers live and die by word counts and deadlines.

That said, my journey took me to farms and kitchens all over the state; a choose-your-own-adventure that was mapped out organically by word-of-mouth referrals from farm to farm, farm to chef, chef to farm, and chef to chef. It was a magical way to experience Maine, and I am so grateful to all the people who wrote out directions or connected me with their farming and cooking friends.

For me, this was a project like none I've tackled before: a collaboration with recipe developers and testers, a chef/photographer, and an international food photography company. If it sounds weird to you, imagine being in the middle of it. But Shannon Day of StockFood made it all seem totally normal. And do-able. Even in the middle of a global pandemic and national civil crises. Ultimately, she is the reason this book is in your hands.

INTRODUCTION

I arrived in Maine in the summer of 2000, a California-born nomad, fresh from a six-month trek wandering east along the highways of America. My husband Steve and I had traveled as far as the roads would take us, stopping only by Maine's jagged coastline to watch the white-capped expanse of ocean engulf our eastward horizon. For Steve, it was a quiet return home to a state that had captured his heart as an undergrad at the University of Maine in the early 1990s. For me, it was as good a place as any to start carving out a career in food—a career that I naïvely believed began and ended with my own skills as a cook, and had little to do with the land and people and culture around me.

My first job was in the newly built kitchen of our local food co-op in Blue Hill, Maine, a sparkling coastal village whose year-round residents supported themselves not only by harvesting lobster and clams, but also by farming the remarkably fertile, loose-soiled land to the north. The new cafe was meant to highlight the fruits, vegetables, and meats that local farmers brought to the co-op's doors on a daily basis.

Having lived almost my entire life on the northern California coast, I was no stranger to farm-to-table cooking. But growing up, these were culinary programs adopted by restaurants that were not only out of reach of my family's budget, but far from the experience of most cooks working the prep stations and the cooking line in most full-service restaurants. The majority of my own professional kitchen experience in California was prepping and cooking produce and meats delivered in the gigantic tractor trailer trucks of national food distributors.

On my first day in the kitchen of a humble Maine food

co-op, I met and shook the hands of a half dozen farmers, young and old, who delivered produce picked from their fields that very morning. Suddenly, unwittingly and without credential, I was welcomed into the fold. What had once seemed an exclusive club of cooks was, in Maine, simply the way we did business. Without asking for it, and because I had landed arbitrarily in our nation's easternmost state, I was gifted the privilege to work with the best, the freshest, and the most nutritious ingredients on the planet—ingredients grown in my own backyard.

It was in that first crowded little kitchen of the Blue Hill Co-op that I began to learn that cooking was less a skill of trade and more an exercise of being present. I talked to growers about their favorite meals prepared in their farm kitchens and started to create simple recipes based on their advice.

Twenty years have passed since those first introductions to Maine's farmers and gardeners. In the last two decades, my culinary education has been augmented by the comprehensive knowledge of fishermen, oyster farmers, hunters, wild food foragers, dairy farmers, and homesteaders. I've received the best instructions on how to cook a beet, a chicken, or a squash from the people who grow and raise these vegetables and animals for our tables. I've found that the most delicious way to enjoy a meal of lobster is steamed over an open fire and nearest to the body of water it was pulled from. And that the best raspberry pie is created in a farm kitchen, on the coldest, darkest days of winter, when the smell of summer fruit pulls us from the brink of longing and fills our hearts with anticipation and hope for the coming season.

My goal in writing this book is to share that knowledge

with you. You'll meet people like Nonesuch Oyster Farm founder Abigail Carroll, who grows pearly-shelled beauties meant to be eaten raw and ice-cold with minced shallot and a few drops of champagne vinegar. Or Beth Schiller, a four-season vegetable farmer in Bowdoinham who grows arugula and cucumbers and herbs so full of flavor and texture that the best way to prepare them is, well, not at all. Clara Coleman, daughter of famed gardener Eliot Coleman, is tilling a path toward the future of her family's Cape Rosier farm. And homesteader and dairy farmer Heather Retberg, whose passionate work for food sovereignty is shining a light on the necessity for small family farms to be allowed to sell their home-raised meat and dairy to their neighbors, not only to alleviate rural food deserts, but also to keep our state's farming traditions alive and viable.

Inside this book, you'll find recipes from these farmers and chefs, like South Paw Farm's Meg Mitchell's Sweet Onion Pie (page 101), or UNION restaurant's Pan-Seared Local Hake with Littleneck Clams, Bok Choy, Chinese-Fermented Sausage, and Soy Brown Butter (page 185). You'll read about Luke's Lobster co-founder Ben Conniff's favorite way to prepare a lobster roll. And you'll learn how a recipe for Acadian buckwheat ployes saved a six-generation family farm in Aroostook County. You'll also find recipes created collaboratively with a team of talented cooks, which highlight the very best the shores, forests, and farms of Maine have to offer; recipes like Sautéed Wild Mushrooms with Thyme (page 188), Grilled Halibut with Spiced Butter Sauce and Snow Peas (page 180), Filet Mignon with Peppered Pears (page 122), and dozens more.

But best of all, you'll be guided from the comfort of your armchair or kitchen on a tour across the width and breadth of Maine; a state made of rocky shores, dark forests, and sharp-angled light. And home to farmers, foragers, and harvesters as textured and diverse as the food they grow.

FROM THE MILL

After a long hiatus in commercial grain production, Maine's Somerset and Aroostook County farmlands are experiencing an agricultural renaissance as forward-thinking farmers respond to an increasing demand for locally grown wheat, corn, rye, and barley. Maine's grain resurgence is largely due to the growth of both the craft beer and artisanal baking industry, while civic-minded entrepreneurs are rebuilding milling infrastructure that disappeared after most of the country's grain production moved west at the beginning of the 19th century.

Northern Maine farmers traditionally rotate grain crops with potatoes, but either till them under, or process them for livestock feed. In recent years, however, these same farmers have been able to sell grain crops to a growing number of local mills, who are, in turn, providing fresh-milled grains to artisanal bakers and brewers.

Freshly milled grains are higher in nutrients and offer far more flavor than highly processed white flours. And these are qualities that can be built upon by skilled bakers who use slow fermentation methods for crusty sourdoughs and multi-grain bread varieties. This chapter explores all the homemade fun you can enjoy with Maine-inspired grain recipes, from breakfast treats to luscious loaves of fresh bread.

MAINE GRAINS AND THE SOMERSET GRIST MILL

SKOWHEGAN

In 2007, friends Amber Lambke and Michael Scholz helped start the Kneading Conference in Skowhegan, bringing together farmers, bakers, millers, and wood-fired oven builders in order to facilitate discussions about reviving Maine's lost grain economy. Inspired by the burgeoning "locavore" movement in Maine and buoyed by the willingness of farmers and bakers to grow and use local grain, the friends concluded that a local grain economy needed a local mill.

Once known as the "Bread Basket of New England," Somerset County produced up to 239,000 bushels of wheat per year, enough to feed more than 100,000 people. But then modernization and the destruction of important infrastruc-

ture destroyed the grain industry in the county, and by 1948, grain production in rural Maine disappeared.

When the vacated Somerset County Jail in downtown Skowhegan went up for sale, Amber and Michael began to not only imagine the future home of a local mill, but also a way to revive their town's depressed economy. Suddenly, their idea to solve a very specific problem in the agricultural economy turned into a big idea—a vision of a thriving downtown food hub, providing jobs, and thus revitalizing an entire impoverished economy. Together, they pooled their resources and bought the building in 2009.

Step by step—forming partnerships, peer-to-peer alliances, and fundraising along the way—Maine Grains was able to purchase a brand-new Austrian-built stone mill and started milling their first shipments of Maine-grown grain in 2012.

Today, Maine Grains produces almost two dozen milled organic grain products, and their product line grows every year. They purchase from over 40 organic farms in Maine and, as of 2019, over one million pounds of local grain has been processed through the mill. They supply over 300 "lead" customers—bakeries, brewers, chefs—from Maine to New York City. Their Dry Goods Shop, opened in 2016, forms the cornerstone of the Somerset Grist Mill Building, now home to the Skowhegan Farmers' Market, a yarn shop, creamery, radio station, and their sister cafe, The Miller's Table.

And most important, the mill and the cafe have created over 30 jobs, and the entire project has been an example of how a community can come together to solve one problem—and many others in the process.

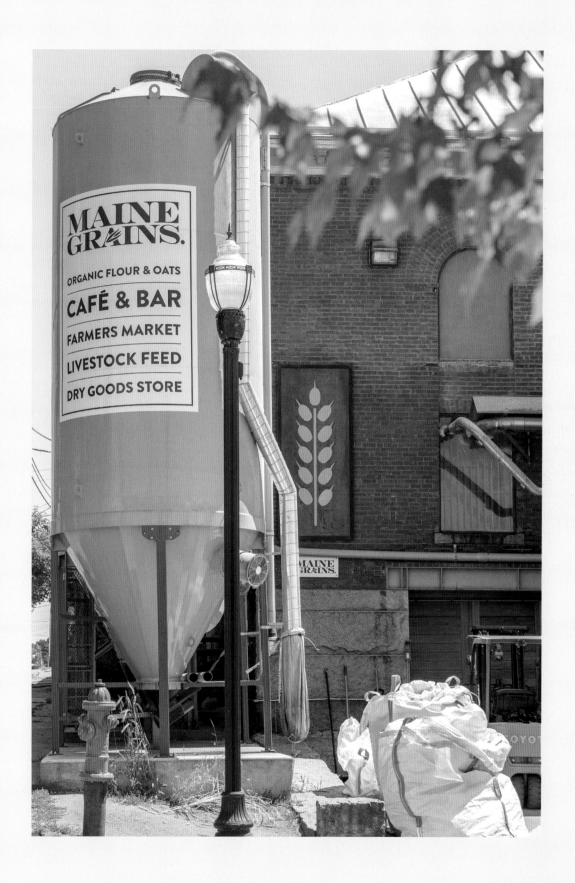

Maine Grains
Maple Granola

MAKES ROUGHLY 4 POUNDS

This recipe makes a delightfully crisp, non-clumpy granola that's hard not to snack on. Yes, four pounds is a lot of granola. But you'll be happy you didn't halve the recipe once you try it.

2 pounds 4 ounces rolled oats

4 ounces raw halved almonds

4 ounces raw pumpkin seeds

4 ounces raw sunflower seeds

4 ounces raw pecans

3 teaspoons baking soda

8 ounces unsalted butter, melted

4 ounces dark brown sugar

4 ounces maple sugar

4 ounces honey

3½ ounces canola oil or olive oil

1 teaspoon sea salt

1¼ pounds dried currants (optional)

1. Preheat the oven to 350°F.

2. In a large bowl, combine the oats, almonds, pumpkin seeds, sunflower seeds, pecans, and baking soda.

3. In a separate bowl, whisk together the melted butter, brown sugar, maple sugar, honey, oil, and salt.

4. Pour the butter-sugar mixture into the oat-nut mixture and stir well.

5. Scrape the granola onto a sheet pan and spread evenly. Bake for 30 minutes, or until golden brown, turning the pan and stirring the granola every 10 minutes. Allow the granola to cool, then stir in the currants if using. Store in an airtight container.

BOUCHARD FAMILY FARMS

FORT KENT

It wasn't all that long ago that the Bouchard family were one of forty potato farms in Fort Kent, which made up a big part of the backbone of Maine agriculture. But when the potato market took a serious dive in the early 80s, and their friends and neighbors began to lose their farms, the family found themselves turning to their French Acadian heritage for a solution.

The Bouchards have been farming 1,000 acres in Aroostook County for six generations.

"With that kind of legacy, no one wants to be the one to lose it," says Janice Bouchard, wife to 5th generation farmer Joe Bouchard.

"My sister-in-law Claire took a trip to Louisiana and came back with beignet mix," Janice recounts. "And she thought, why hasn't anyone done this with ployes?"

Ployes, a crêpe-like pancake made from buckwheat flour, are, like beignets, a French Acadian staple. But unlike the tiny pillow-like doughnut made famous by New Orleans's Cafe du Monde, ployes were virtually unknown outside of northern Maine.

So the Bouchard sisters got to work and developed a recipe for an easy-to-use mix and began to package it out of their home kitchen.

Meanwhile, Joe and his father Alban began converting their land from potatoes to buckwheat. And by 1997, they were self-milling their buckwheat on the farm with a rebuilt 19th century mill they brought from Canada.

Janice says that the ploye business is credited with having saved the family farm, and has since inspired other on-farm innovations, including a

year-round country store that sells market produce, meats, crafts, greenhouse plants, and, of course, all the Bouchard Family Farms packaged ploye mixes and buckwheat flour.

According to Janice, a large part of their business is driven by the rising demand for gluten-free products.

Today the farm, which is operated by Janice, Joe, their son Philip, Alban (now in his 90s), and one other employee, has two to three hundred acres in buckwheat, oats, and hay for a handful of cattle, and 25 acres in organic potatoes.

"It's hard to get potatoes out of my husband's blood," Janice says.

Ployes

MAKES 14 TO 20

The Bouchards sell their traditional ployes mix directly from their farm and website, but you can also find it in grocery stores all over Maine and New England. However, if you would like to try your hand at making ployes from scratch, this recipe comes straight from the well-worn pages of the Bouchards' family cookbook. Traditionally, *les ployes* are never flipped to cook on both sides. And they are often served bubble-side up, bearing a striking resemblance to the Ethiopian flatbread, injera. If you've never had ployes, you're in for a treat that will likely become a staple accompaniment to meals from maple syrup breakfasts to dinnertime soups and stews.

½ cup light buckwheat flour

½ cup all-purpose wheat flour

2½ teaspoons baking powder

½ teaspoon sea salt

1⅓ cups cold water

1. In a medium-size bowl, mix the dry ingredients together. Add the cold water to the bowl and beat until there are no lumps in the batter. Let the batter sit for about 5 minutes.

2. While the batter rests, heat a griddle or cast-iron pan to about 400°F.

3. When the griddle is hot, pour 2 to 3 tablespoons of batter onto the hot, ungreased surface. Spread the batter out in a circular motion with the back of a spoon.

4. Cook the ployes on one side only for about 90 seconds, or until the surface of the ployes is bubbled and set.

5. Remove the ployes from the griddle and flip onto a plate. Serve with good, fresh butter and Maine maple syrup.

AURORA MILLS & FARM

LINNEUS

In the 1990s, University of Maine agronomist Matt Williams started growing organic wheat on his Aroostook County farm at the suggestion of Borealis Breads founder Jim Amaral. Matt later started milling the grain on-site, thus setting Maine's grain renaissance in motion.

Matt's daughter Sara Williams Flewelling and her husband Marcus joined the farm in 2013. They have helped grow product lines and distribution and have plans to expand the milling operation to nearby Houlton. Aurora produces and mills several varieties of wheat, oats, rye, buckwheat, and spelt—some exclusively for restaurants and breweries. The farm continues to partner with Borealis Breads, as well as other well-known Maine companies such as Allagash Brewing Company and GrandyOats.

Classic Popovers

MAKES 6

Popovers depend on steam for their quick, high rise, so for baking success, make sure you allow the oven to get up to temperature before you bake the popovers. And no matter how tempting it is, don't open that oven door while they're baking! Doing so will likely interfere with the rising, and you'll end up with a deflated, dense pastry.

3 teaspoons canola or sunflower oil

1¼ cups all-purpose flour

¼ teaspoon sea salt

1 pinch ground black pepper

2 eggs, beaten

1⅓ cups milk

1. Preheat the oven to 425°F. Place a 6-cavity popover pan on top of a baking sheet.

2. Grease the popover tray with the oil, then place the pan in the oven while you make the batter.

3. Whisk together the flour, sea salt, and pepper in a medium-size bowl.

4. Beat the eggs into the flour mixture until blended, then gradually beat in the milk until smooth.

5. Divide the batter evenly between the smoking hot cavities of the popover pan and bake for 10 to 15 minutes, or until well-risen and puffy. Serve immediately.

Corn Pancakes

SERVES 4

These pancakes are meant to be a savory dish, but they are just as good with maple syrup and butter as they are with sour cream and parmesan cheese. Even the basil goes well with either the savory or sweet variation. Although the recipe calls for fine cornmeal, I have made these with coarser stone-ground varieties and love the nubbly texture and fuller flavor.

1¾ cups fine cornmeal

¼ cup cornstarch

1 teaspoon granulated sugar

1 teaspoon baking soda

½ teaspoon sea salt

1¾ cups buttermilk

2 large eggs

4 tablespoons canola oil

½ cup fresh or frozen corn kernels

4 tablespoons sour cream, for serving

2 tablespoons grated Parmesan, for serving

2 tablespoons thinly sliced fresh
    basil leaves, for serving

1. Whisk together the cornmeal, cornstarch, sugar, baking soda, and salt in a large mixing bowl.

2. Whisk together the buttermilk, eggs, and oil in a separate mixing bowl. Stir in the corn.

3. Stir the wet ingredients into the dry ingredients until just combined.

4. Preheat a large non-stick frying pan over a medium heat until hot. Slick the pan with a little canola oil.

5. Scoop the batter in ¼-cup increments into the hot pan. Let the pancakes set and turn golden underneath, about 1 to 2 minutes. Flip and cook until golden-brown on the other side, about 1 to 2 minutes. Slide out onto a plate lined with parchment and loosely cover with foil to keep warm.

6. Repeat for the remaining pancakes, using a little more oil.

7. When ready to serve, stack the pancakes on plates and top with sour cream, grated parmesan, and basil leaves.

Cornmeal Pudding

SERVES 6 TO 8

This rustic, nubbly-textured dessert is an old-fashioned New England staple based on the flour-and-milk pudding recipes early American colonists brought with them from England—often referred to as hasty puddings. This preparation, with the cornmeal made from white flint corn acquired from their Native American neighbors, was an adaptation adopted as a result of the scarcity of wheat in the New World. The dessert is commonly called Indian pudding and is served alongside the pumpkin pie at many a traditional Thanksgiving dinner.

2½ tablespoons unsalted butter

4 cups milk

5 tablespoons fine yellow cornmeal

⅓ cup Maine maple syrup

⅓ cup molasses

1 pinch sea salt

¼ teaspoon ground cinnamon

½ teaspoon ground ginger

½ teaspoon nutmeg

¼ to ½ cup raisins (optional)

1 egg, lightly beaten

Vanilla ice cream or freshly whipped cream, for serving

1. Preheat the oven to 300° F. Grease a 1½ quart baking or casserole dish with 1 tablespoon butter. Set aside.

2. Heat 3 cups of the milk and the remaining butter in a saucepan until the mixture comes to a boil. Add the cornmeal in a slow stream, whisking to prevent clumping. Reduce the heat to low. Stir for about 5 minutes or until the mixture thickens.

3. Remove the pan from the heat.

4. Whisk together the maple syrup, molasses, salt, cinnamon, ginger, nutmeg, raisins (if using), and egg in a medium, heatproof bowl. Pour a little of the hot milk mixture into the syrup-spice mixture while whisking. Then pour the tempered mixture back into the hot milk mixture and whisk to combine.

5. Pour the pudding into the prepared baking dish and bake for 30 minutes.

6. Pour the remaining cold milk over the pudding and return it to the oven. Continue baking for 1½ to 1¾ hours, or until the top is well-browned.

7. Serve the pudding warm with a scoop of vanilla ice cream or whipped cream.

SONGBIRD FARMS

UNITY

For Johanna Davis and Adam Nordell, grains were part of the farming equation from the beginning. Starting out on 3 acres of borrowed land in midcoast Maine in 2010, the couple grew Hopi blue corn alongside dried bean crops and market vegetables.

From those first crops in 2010 that they traded for rent, Johanna and Adam went on to participate in the MOFGA Journeyperson Program and expanded their grain and wholesale vegetable production on Sweet Land Farm in Starks. It was there, that Songbird Farms started one of the first grain and wheat CSAs in Maine.

Today, the couple cultivates 20 acres of diversified crops in Unity, including heritage grains such as rye, oats, several different kinds of wheat, and the Abenaki Flint corn for which they are locally famous. They mill all their grains on-site with a stone mill purchased from Maine Grains Alliance and funded by an Indiegogo campaign.

They sell their grains to a few local restaurants and as part of their popular "Pantry Share CSA," which provides home bakers with a winter's worth of fresh-milled grains at the end of each harvest season in October.

Brown Bread

MAKES 2 COFFEE CAN-SIZE LOAVES OR ONE 9-INCH LOAF

When she was feeling homesick, my East Coast-born mother would bring home B&M Baked Beans and canned brown bread from the forgotten aisles of our northern California grocery store, and we would indulge in the molasses-y flavors of her youth. Having now lived in Maine for over 20 years, I rarely see home cooks making brown bread and can't help but wonder why. It's simple, satisfying, and delicious! You can find tube-shaped pudding molds to stand in for coffee cans for traditionally shaped brown bread. Or you can completely break from tradition and use any fancy pudding mold you have on hand.

1 to 2 tablespoons butter

1 cup all-purpose white flour

1 cup rye flour

1 cup fine cornmeal

2 teaspoons baking soda

1 teaspoon sea salt

⅔ cup dark molasses

2 cups milk

1 cup raisins (optional)

1. Preheat the oven to 325°F. Grease 2 one-pound coffee cans and one side of a sheet of aluminum foil with butter. If you don't have coffee cans, use a 9-inch loaf pan.

2. In a mixing bowl, whisk together the white flour, rye flour, cornmeal, baking soda, and salt.

3. In a large measuring cup, stir together the molasses and milk. Pour this mixture into the dry ingredients and stir well. Fold in the raisins, if using.

4. Scrape the batter into the buttered cans or loaf pan. Cover the top with the buttered foil.

5. Place the cans or loaf pan in a large roasting pan and place the dish in the oven. Before closing the oven door, carefully pour boiling water into the roasting pan so that it comes about halfway up the side of the cans or loaf pan.

6. Bake for 1 hour 45 minutes, topping up the hot water as needed if it starts to run dry. When ready, a skewer or knife will come out clean from the center of the bread.

7. Remove the cans/loaf pan to a cooling rack, letting the bread cool completely in the can. Turn out, slice, and serve.

Pan-Baked Corn Bread

SERVES 4

I grew up on the floury, cake-sweet cornbreads that required no more work than mixing milk and egg into a powdered mix from a cardboard box. Stoneground cornmeal in all its forms—coarse, fine, white, blue, yellow, even red!—was, for me, an adult revelation. Most of the cornmeals coming from local mills in Maine are coarsely ground and, even though this recipe calls for "fine cornmeal," I encourage you to also try the coarser grinds as well. They can turn this easy cornbread into an artisan baked good, richly textured and exploding with unexpected flavor.

1⅓ cups all-purpose flour

1 cup fine yellow cornmeal

¼ cup granulated sugar

2 teaspoons baking powder

1 teaspoon baking soda

½ teaspoon salt

1 cup buttermilk

⅓ cup vegetable oil

2 large eggs, lightly beaten

1 green onion, green tops only, sliced

1 tablespoon butter

1. Preheat the oven to 400°F.

2. Stir together the flour, cornmeal, sugar, baking powder, baking soda, and salt in a large mixing bowl.

3. Add the buttermilk, vegetable oil, and eggs, and mix until the batter is just combined. It shouldn't be totally smooth; some lumps are OK. Stir in the sliced green onions.

4. Place the butter in a 10-inch cast-iron skillet set over a moderate heat. Heat until melted and frothy. Pour in the batter, spread it to the edges of the pan, and cook it on the stovetop for two minutes before transferring it to the oven.

5. Bake the cornbread for 25 to 30 minutes, until puffed and golden on top; a toothpick should come out clean from its center.

6. Remove from the oven and let cool briefly before serving.

Buttermilk Biscuits

SERVES 6

If you are able, use freshly milled sifted wheat flour and locally produced butter for this recipe. If you're lucky enough to find yourself in Maine, local mills such as Maine Grains and artisanal butter producers like Casco Bay Creamery, as well as small dairy farms at a local farmers' market, are great resources for ultra-fresh premium ingredients. But no matter where you are, sourcing local ingredients for even the simplest of dishes, like these biscuits, is sure to bring fresh flavor to any meal. Here, locally milled flour and butter elevate this from a simple quick bread to something worth showing off to company.

**1¾ cups sifted wheat flour or white all-
    purpose flour, plus extra for dusting**

¼ teaspoon baking powder

¾ teaspoon baking soda

1 teaspoon granulated sugar

½ teaspoon salt

**¼ cup unsalted butter, cold and cubed,
    plus 1 tablespoon melted butter**

¾ cup buttermilk

1. Preheat the oven to 350°F. Line a large baking sheet with parchment paper.

2. Sift the flour, baking powder, baking soda, sugar, and salt into a mixing bowl. Stir to combine.

3. Add the cubed butter and rub into the flour mixture until pea-sized pieces of butter and flour form. Gently stir in the buttermilk with a spatula until a rough dough forms; it shouldn't be totally smooth.

4. Dust a work surface with some flour. Place the dough on top and sprinkle with more flour before flattening out into a ½-inch thick round.

5. Cut out 2½-inch wide rounds with a large cookie cutter, approximately six in total. Arrange on the baking sheet and brush with the melted butter.

6. Bake the biscuits until risen and golden-brown, 15 to 20 minutes, rotating the sheet halfway through baking.

7. Remove when ready and let cool briefly on the sheet before serving warm.

TORTILLERÍA PACHANGA

PORTLAND

When Lynne Rowe was gifted a wooden tortilla press while she was living in rural Mexico in her 20s, she could have never guessed that it would lead to her starting a tortilla factory two decades later in Maine.

Lynne met her husband, Jon, while they were both teaching in Portland. It was while the couple was living and teaching in Mexico as newlyweds that a student's mother gave Lynne a traditional wooden tortilla press and taught Lynne to make tortillas—a Mexican pantry staple—from fresh masa.

Tortilla-making—and the wooden press—followed Lynne as she and her husband returned to and eventually settled in Maine where Lynne continued her career as a Spanish language teacher, which culminated ultimately as the World Language Coordinator for Portland Public Schools.

Lynne spent hours in her home kitchen figuring out how to nixtamalize corn by soaking the kernels in a 1-percent lime solution—a process that is necessary to dissolve the outer hard-to-digest hull of the corn kernels. The process also softened the hard grains so that she could grind them into a stiff dough, known as masa. Lynne taught her Spanish language students how to make tortillas from the fresh masa and eventually she decided it was time to take the leap into professional tortilla making.

Today, Tortillería Pachanga is one of only a few tortilla factories in the northeast, and the only one in Maine. Lynne sources organic corn from a network of Maine farms, and makes her fresh masa and tortillas from organic dent corn, as well as heritage varieties such as Bloody Butcher, Somali Flint, and Abenaki Flint. Her partnership with the Somali Bantu community at Liberation Farms in Wales, Maine, has resulted in a tortilla made with a blend of dent corn and the farm's Somali flint corn.

Partnering with other Maine businesses that also make perishable products, Lynne operates a refrigerated delivery service from Portland, making fresh tortilla deliveries to restaurants and grocery stores throughout the state of Maine.

Tortillería Pachanga Chorizo Molotes

MAKES 24 MOLOTES

Molotes are a Mexican street food that can be found typically in Oaxaca and Puebla. They can be found in many shapes and sizes, from a half-moon (similar to an empanada) to little balls like hush puppies. The most traditional is a sort of cigar or torpedo shape. Lynne Rowe, owner of Tortillería Pachanga, prefers the half-moon shape for the super-thin, extra-crispy edges you end up with.

The one thing all versions of molotes have in common is that they are made with a base of corn masa. We add a bit of oil and salt to the masa to make the dough easy to work with, extra crunchy on the outside, and to bring out the flavor of the corn. Molotes can be filled with an endless list of tasty and varied fillings, but here we are sticking with the most popular one of chorizo and potato. You can make this a vegetarian version with soy-based chorizo. Molotes are amazing with all kinds of toppings: Mexican crema, salsa of your choice, a sprinkle of cotija cheese, pickled red onions—the list is endless. ¡Buen provecho!

Masa

2 pounds fresh masa (see Tip)

2 tablespoons canola or sunflower oil

¼ teaspoon salt

Filling

1 pound chorizo (or substitute)

1 pound potatoes (your favorite kind)

8 ounces shredded sharp cheddar cheese

1. To make the masa: Knead the masa with the oil and salt until smooth and workable. You might want to add a bit of water to the masa to get it nice and moist (if it seems a bit dried out) before adding the oil and optional water. Divide the prepared masa into 24 golfball-sized balls.

2. To make the filling: In a frying pan, cook the chorizo until it is cooked through. Drain off some of the fat. In a large pot of water, bring the potatoes to a boil and cook until they are fork tender. Cut them up in cubes and add to the chorizo and mix well. Don't worry if the potato ends up a bit mashed. Taste and add some salt if needed. Allow the mixture to cool.

3. Using a tortilla press, two plates, or two other flat items and a heavy plastic bag cut in half, press out the masa balls into circles of about 5½ inches in diameter (you can make them thicker or thinner depending on your preference). Pull one side of the plastic off the top and lay an ounce or so of filling plus a few pinches of cheese on one side of the circle. Use the plastic bag to lay one half of the masa over the filled side and push down to seal the edges. You can assemble your molotes ahead of time and keep them on a cookie sheet with a damp cloth on top to keep them from drying out.

4. In a heavy frying pan, heat about 2 inches of oil to 375°F. Fry the molotes in batches, about 2 to 3 minutes per side, until they are golden and crispy. Drain on a paper towel and add your favorite toppings or dip in your favorite sauce.

Tip: If you can find fresh masa from 100-percent Nixtamal, you will notice the difference. But you will still end up with something super yummy if you use the equivalent amount of masa made from dried masa harina.

NIGHT MOVES BREAD + PIE

BIDDEFORD

For Kerry Hanney, founder and head baker at Night Moves Bread + Pie, bread making was the culmination of her search for a sustainable, art-filled, health-based way of life.

Trained as a sculptor, Kerry found she wasn't interested in gallery life and instead craved a path that connected her with her community, supported her local economy, and promoted a healthy lifestyle.

She spent years in bakeries up and down the Eastern Seaboard, learning the ins and outs of American-style pastry and the schedules of various different kinds of bakeries. Eventually she turned to bread as her medium.

"I was drawn to the natural rhythms of bread baking and the intuitive sense of timing," Kerry says. "And learning to trust that intuition."

Kerry's breads are naturally leavened, slowly fermented, and made with stone-ground grains. This process, and the ingredients she uses, ensure optimal nutrition and a long shelf-life without the use of stabilizers. As she worked and learned alongside seasoned bakers, Kerry eventually began to trust her own baking intuition and set out to find a kitchen of her own in Maine.

"The guiding force of this business is Maine-grown grains," Kerry explains. "The flavor potential and health benefits are amazing."

Kerry founded Night Moves Bread + Pie in 2016, with the intention of supporting the local grain economy, making delicious, healthful bread and baked goods crafted from locally grown grains accessible to her community, and creating a desirable work environment for her and her employees.

"Part of this whole project for me is creating a

sustainable work/life balance, and trying to do things a different way," Kerry explains. "I saw too much turnover in bakeries as a result of crazy schedules."

Kerry saw the greatest potential for a sustainable baking schedule with a wholesale business model.

Night Moves currently makes seven types of breads, seasonal pies, one type of cookie, and one type of brownie—all from 100 percent locally grown stone-milled grain, local dairy and butter, and Maine-grown produce. The bakery's products are available for sale at just over a dozen retail outlets and are served at the tables of a handful of southern Maine restaurants. Well-planning customers can also order online for a scheduled pick-up at the bakery.

As Night Moves grows, Kerry finds that her vision is evolving at a similar pace, and she sees an opportunity for more retail while still retaining a sustainable schedule.

"I love that direct connection with my customers," she says.

In 2019, Night Moves launched a storefront in the renovated Pepperill Mill in Biddeford, and is open to the public two days a week.

TINDER HEARTH

BROOKSVILLE

"The bakery is our first child," says Lydia Moffet, co-owner, with her husband Tim Semler, of Tinder Hearth. The business is centered around a big wood-fired oven on a family homestead in a forested pocket of the Blue Hill Peninsula. Lydia and Tim, who now have two other children (of the human variety), started Tinder Hearth out of a desire to make an essential contribution to their community while working as part of a close-knit group.

Tinder Hearth specializes in long-fermented sourdough bread—loaves, batards, boules, and miche—that make use of fresh, flavorful organic flours from Maine and Quebec. It's the kind of bread that contains equal parts grain and spirit—a soulful piece of each team member that kneaded, shaped, and fired each loaf.

Since the couple and a small group of friends started making bread in 2007, Tinder Hearth has grown from a bakery that produced enough loaves for local barter and the farmers' market, to an essential community service that produces not only bread, but butter croissants, pizza, and an assortment of other pastries—all from their big, brick, wood-fired oven.

In the summer, the gardens on the family's property turn into an outside pizza restaurant, where the community comes to gather and enjoy fresh salads and oven-crisped pizzas made with vegetables from nearby Four Season Farm, meats

from small farms on the Blue Hill Peninsula, and locally sourced cheeses. The hand-stretched, flavorful crusts are made with a poolish enhanced with a healthy starter.

And while the locally grown foods that make up the bakery's breads, pizzas, and pastries are a big piece of the equation, Lydia feels that the most important ingredient comes from the nucleus of the bakery itself. "Our team means everything, and we believe that good food requires good vibes in the kitchen."

The bakery employs eight people year-round, and as many as 30 in the summer months.

"We work hard with the young folks who come seasonally to work with us," Lydia says. "Both to teach them how to make excellent food and also how to work collectively with heart." She says she feels pride in watching these young people grow beyond their summer jobs at Tinder Hearth, and hopes that she and her core team have contributed in a small way to how they carry themselves into their future lives and labors.

"To have work that matters," says Lydia. "To be believed in to grow and succeed, to be a part of a supportive and challenging team, and to be seen . . . is . . . important."

Tinder Hearth's Sourdough Whole Spelt Bread

MAKES 3 LOAVES

Lydia Moffet, co-owner of Tinder Hearth Bakery, says that freshly milled whole spelt flour makes a world of difference for this simple, no-knead sourdough bread. You will need a healthy, active starter to complete this recipe.

Levain

2¾ ounces sourdough starter
2¾ ounces water, at 80°F
2¾ ounces whole spelt flour

Dough

2¾ pounds water, at 80°F
1¼ ounces sea salt
3⅛ pounds whole spelt flour

1. To make the levain: Using a happy sourdough starter that was refreshed the previous night, combine the starter, water, and whole spelt flour in a small bowl. Cover the bowl with a cloth and let the levain rest in a very warm room (80°F is ideal) for 2 hours. You want it to be young but active, with just a touch of "sea-foam" around the rim.

2. To make the dough: Remove a pinch of your levain and mix it into your original starter before you put it away. Then place the remaining levain, the water, sea salt, and spelt flour in a large bowl. Mix well, working out any lumps with your fingers. It should feel like a batter: wet and gloppy.

3. Cover the bowl with a cloth and let the dough proof for 4 hours. For the first 2 hours, "turn" the dough every 30 minutes. Do this by scooping the dough up with lightly floured hands and letting it drop down and fold over itself.

4. Divide the dough into 3 well-oiled pans—no shaping necessary. Just plop them in there.

5. Let the dough proof in the pans for 4 hours.

6. When ready to bake the loaves, preheat the oven to 400°F.

7. Bake the loaves for 45 minutes.

8. Let the loaves sit for 1 minute before popping them out to cool on a rack.

Tip: If you prefer to bake in the morning, the shaped loaves can sit overnight in a 40°F room or the refrigerator. Bake them straight-away in the morning; no need to proof longer.

THE MILLER'S TABLE AT MAINE GRAINS

SKOWHEGAN

There is a community table in the old rec yard of the old county jail in Skowhegan that is dubbed the Miller's Table, and on any given night, you'll find a convivial gathering of community members enjoying a meal of bubbly-crusted wood-fired pizzas and hyper local salads. Inside—in the old jail garage bay—there is a cozy dining room. Here, diners are served meals crafted from produce grown at neighboring farms and baked goods made from grains milled at the on-site gristmill, Maine Grains.

A jail might be an unlikely model for community growth, but when Amber Lambke purchased the building in 2009 to be the future home of Maine Grains (page 18), she led the way for an economic renaissance in a part of Maine that could really use it.

The Miller's Table, also started by Lambke, serves a menu of comfort foods and pizzas, featuring local organic grains milled on-site. The pizzas, made with a naturally fermented dough produced by the bakery across the street (which uses flours from the mill), are thin-crusted tributes to area farms, loaded with sausages, vegetables, fruits, and cheeses all produced in Maine. Slung by local teens, the pizzas also serve as the vehicle for the restaurant's fundraising program, Pizza with a Purpose, which gives a generous portion of pizza sales on a single evening to local non-profits.

Potato Pizza with Olives and Fresh Oregano

SERVES 4

Pizza crust is basically a simple flatbread made from very few ingredients, so using freshly milled whole grain flour will improve flavor and texture. For this recipe, even a combination of all-purpose white flour and sifted whole wheat flours will add complexity and interest to the simple crust. And when in Maine, add potatoes to everything, including pizza. The tender, buttery flesh of fingerlings save this carb on carb pizza from boring indulgence. Fingerlings aren't great storage potatoes, so find them fresh in late summer through the fall at local farm stands and farmers' markets. Thinly slice them with the help of a mandoline if you have one, for a pleasingly crunchy topping.

Basic Pizza Dough

2¼ cups all-purpose flour, plus extra for dusting

1¾ teaspoons active dry yeast

1 teaspoon sea salt

3 tablespoons extra-virgin olive oil, plus extra for oiling and drizzling

¾ cup warm water (approximately 110°F)

Toppings

4 large fingerling potatoes

1 cup shredded mozzarella

½ cup roughly chopped pitted green olives

¼ cup fresh oregano sprigs

1. To make the Basic Pizza Dough: Combine the flour, yeast, and salt in a large mixing bowl. Add the olive oil, mix briefly, and then stir in the water, bringing the mixture together into a rough dough with your hands.

2. Turn out onto a floured surface and knead until smooth and elastic, 6 to 8 minutes. Place in a clean, oiled bowl and cover loosely. Leave to rise for 30 minutes in a warm place.

3. Preheat the oven to 475°F. Place a large baking sheet or pizza stone in the oven to preheat.

4. Punch down the risen dough. Roll out on a lightly floured surface into a ¼-inch-thick round or oval.

5. To make the toppings: Lift the dough onto a floured piece of parchment paper. Finely slice the potatoes using a mandoline, arranging them on the dough, overlapping as needed.

6. Scatter the mozzarella and olives on top. Drizzle with some olive oil and slide the pizza onto the baking sheet or pizza stone.

7. Bake for 10 to 12 minutes until the dough has risen and is golden brown at the edges; the cheese should be golden and bubbling.

8. Remove from the oven and let cool before topping with oregano and serving.

Rustic Tomato Pizza

SERVES 4

If you don't like red sauce on your pizza but LOVE fresh, in-season tomatoes, this is the pie for you. This is a candidate for showcasing the rainbow assortment of late summer and early fall tomatoes. Choose tomatoes of varying sizes and slice them thinly so that your pizza doesn't get soggy.

Basic Pizza Dough (page 46)

Cornmeal, for sprinkling

6 teaspoons extra virgin olive oil

½ cup prepared basil pesto

1½ pounds mixed heirloom or other seasonal tomatoes, thinly sliced

Fine sea salt, to taste

Freshly ground black pepper, to taste

1 handful fresh baby arugula

1. Prepare the Basic Pizza Dough and leave it to rise for at least 30 minutes in a warm place.

2. Position one oven rack in the center and one rack on the bottom of the oven and preheat to 450°F. Sprinkle cornmeal over a baking sheet. Punch down and roll out the dough into a ¼-inch-thick round or oval. Transfer the dough to the prepared baking sheet.

3. Drizzle 2 teaspoons of oil over the pizza dough. Spread half of the prepared pesto over the pizza dough, leaving a 1-inch border from the edge. Arrange the tomato slices in a single layer and drizzle with the remaining pesto. Season to taste with salt and pepper.

4. Bake for about 15 minutes or until the crust is crisp and brown on the bottom. Arrange the fresh arugula on top of the pizza and drizzle with remaining oil. Cut the pizza into wedges and serve immediately.

FROM THE FIELD

Of Maine's 7,500-plus farms, roughly 1,300 of them grow and harvest vegetables for fresh markets. While potatoes and corn occupy the most acreage, Maine farmers produce over 50 other major crops, plus dozens of other heirloom or small-crop vegetables grown at the request of chefs or other highly specialized markets.

Walk into one of Maine's 115 farmers' markets in late August or early September, and you will find vegetables ranging from tender spring greens such as baby lettuces and dandelion greens to high summer crops such as sweet corn, peppers, and eggplants; for fall storage, you will find vegetables like pumpkins, turnips, and beets. The summer growing season in Maine is short and motley, producing crops in such quick succession that late summer culminates in a harvest of unlikely vegetable bedfellows.

This is, of course, good news for cooks, whose ingredients palette encompasses a vast selection of textures, colors, and flavors, and allows endless possibility for vegetable-centric meals.

DANDELION SPRING FARM

BOWDOINHAM

"I started farming with the idea that it was going to be a perfect metaphor to talk about the other environmental issues that were important to me," says Beth Schiller, founder of Dandelion Spring Farm in Bowdoinham. "Farming just seems like such a perfect way to talk about how we care for the earth. I was very philosophical about it. But I also discovered pretty quickly that I really like the work."

The 30 open acres of her 80-acre farm are host to over 30 crops, including soil grown plants in eight year-round greenhouses. While the farm is probably best known for their tiny jewel-like heads of romaine, tender arugula, cut baby lettuces, fresh herbs, and their namesake dandelion greens, Beth and her team of 10 full- and part-time employees also tend storage crops of carrots, beets, and squashes, as well as highly seasonal plants such as cucumbers, tomatoes, eggplants, and baby zucchinis. About half of Beth's sales are directly to restaurants known for their farm-to-table programs, like Fore Street and Solo Italiano in Portland, and Nīna June and Long Grain on the midcoast.

The other half of her sales comes from the Portland and Rockland farmers' markets, including the winter market in Portland.

Beth says she never imagined that she'd be a four-season farmer when she began her career two decades ago.

"The goal was to make enough money during

the summer so that we didn't have to in the winter." But, she says, thanks to the efforts of organizations like Maine Farmland Trust and Maine Organic Farmers and Gardeners Association (MOFGA), there are so many new farmers in Maine that she feels she has to keep pushing the market to maintain her space. And that's a good thing.

Having served on the board of MOFGA, including a tenure as president from 2019 to 2021, Beth is part of the force that has dedicated countless hours to building the farming population in her home state.

"We still need more locally produced food in Maine," Beth asserts, despite catapulting farming populations in the southern part of the state. "We're not feeding Maine yet."

Beth acknowledges a disparity between the rural counties to the north and the relatively well-heeled communities in the south, and feels that a better conversation between the "two Maines" and more fresh market crops in the northern part of the state would help alleviate the shortage of home-grown food.

"We need to build a bridge between the rural economy and the urban economy," Beth says. "I think food could be that bridge."

Beth Schiller's Wilted Frisée Salad with Ground Lamb and Fresh Chile

SERVES 4

Alongside the dainty honeynut squash, fairy egg-plants, French breakfast radishes, and crate after crate of fresh greens at the Dandelion Spring Farm's stall at the Portland and Rockland Farmers' Markets, Beth keeps a cooler stocked full of Straw's Farm lamb and mutton. Beth actually prefers this recipe with ground mutton. The strong flavors of both the meat and the seasonings blend to an umami crescendo that mingles gracefully with the sharp, somewhat bitter greens.

1 tablespoon extra virgin olive oil

1 large shallot, chopped

1 pound ground lamb or mutton

1 small red jalapeño, sliced into very thin rounds

1 clove garlic, finely chopped

1 tablespoon fish sauce

1 teaspoon (or more to taste) tamari

½ teaspoon toasted sesame oil

1 large head frisée, coarsely chopped

1 head radicchio, coarsely chopped

1½ teaspoons toasted sesame seeds

1. Heat the olive oil in a wide cast-iron skillet over medium heat. Add the chopped shallot and sauté until softened and translucent.

2. Add the ground lamb to the skillet. Brown the meat, breaking it up as it cooks.

3. When the meat is cooked and nicely browned, stir in the jalapeño, garlic, fish sauce, tamari, and sesame oil. Sauté for another minute, then remove the skillet from the heat.

4. Place the chopped frisée and radicchio in a large salad bowl. Scrape the hot lamb mixture over the greens and immediately toss the salad with tongs so that everything is coated with the flavorful dressing.

5. Scatter the toasted sesame seeds over the salad and serve immediately.

Warm Kale Salad with Golden Potatoes

SERVES 4

Although Maine has a relatively short outdoor growing season, an increasing number of farmers are using state-funded programs to invest in greenhouses in order to extend harvests through the winter. Crops like salad greens, kale, and other dark leafy greens are perfect candidates for greenhouse growing and are now readily available year round in Maine. Fall harvest kale—even more tender varieties like the lacinato called for here—is best if it is sliced thinly so that the leaves can tenderize properly in the dressing. And storage crops like potatoes are well suited to the dressing's hearty flavors.

2 pounds yellow-fleshed potatoes, peeled and cut into a 1-inch dice

⅓ cup olive oil

Sea salt, to taste

Freshly ground black pepper, to taste

⅓ cup grated Parmigiano-Reggiano cheese

¼ cup well-stirred tahini

3 tablespoons water

3 tablespoons fresh lemon juice

2 small cloves garlic, crushed

10 ounces curly leafed or lacinato kale, stems and center ribs discarded and leaves very thinly sliced crosswise

1. Preheat the oven to 450°F with rack in upper third.

2. Toss the potatoes with the olive oil, sea salt, and pepper in a large bowl, and then spill them onto a sheet pan and spread them in a single layer. Roast for 20 to 25 minutes, until potatoes are fork-tender and golden brown, stirring once halfway through. Place them back in the large bowl.

3. While the potatoes are roasting, whir the grated cheese, tahini, water, lemon juice, and garlic in a blender or food processor until smooth. Season to taste with salt and pepper.

4. Add the thinly sliced kale to the bowl of roasted potatoes and toss. Add the dressing to the vegetables and toss again so that everything is evenly coated. Season with salt and pepper to taste and serve.

THE SCHOONER *STEPHEN TABER*

ROCKLAND

When passengers board a schooner on the coast of Maine in the summertime, there are no guarantees for glittering days and smooth sailing. In fact, it is more likely that the weather will be . . . well . . . weather: damp, foggy, both too hot and too cold, and always unpredictable.

But when guests board the 148-year-old two-masted *Stephen Taber* at her home berth in Rockland, Maine, there is one sure thing: They will, without a doubt, eat like kings.

Captained by Noah Barnes, who took over the schooner from his parents, the *Stephen Taber* is one of a handful of vessels that hang their laurels on the quality of Maine-grown bounty and the skill of its cooks.

It used to be that the standard fare among Maine's fleet of windjammers reached no higher than hearty chowders, baked beans, and even hamburgers and "red hots" (a neon-hued frankfurter that is a Maine convenience store ubiquity). But with tourists adding Maine to their lists of must-visit culinary destinations due to the reputation of its James Beard Award-winning chefs and brewers, it was only a matter of time before a few forward-thinking captains came to realize the market value of ramping up their vessels' culinary program.

Aboard the *Stephen Taber*, an unflappable galley chef coaxes bistro meals from the 100-year-old wood-fired Clarion stove in a below-deck kitchen the size of most suburban closets.

Dinners begin with charcuterie boards laden with local cheeses, freshly baked bread, and house-cured duck prosciutto and salami—the

result of a two-day winter "duck party" led by long-time schooner chef Anna Miller. Fresh-caught fish, Maine-raised meats, and brightly colored vegetables from Amanda LaBelle's Hope's Edge Farm fill out a never-ending parade of lush meals that begin at sunrise with steaming mugs of locally roasted coffee and end after sundown with flaky-crusted pies and bubbling cobblers. And each trip culminates in a decadent lobster feast on one of Maine's hidden deserted islands, reachable only by water.

"We are unapologetic hedonists," says Captain Noah, of the over-the-top meals aboard his schooner.

Unique among the modern windjamming fleet

are the *Taber*'s expert wine pairings that accompany the meals, courtesy of Noah's wife, Jane Barnes. Jane, a former wine merchant from New York City, left a life of globe-trotting and wine-procuring when she married Noah, a Maine-raised, guitar-strumming, free-spirited sailor. Ellen and Ken Barnes, who ran the schooner for 25 years, passed the torch to Noah and Jane in 2003. Noah said he learned most of how to host what is essentially a week-long on-board house party from his charismatic parents.

"After all," Noah reasons. "If we cannot provide beautiful, jaw-dropping food to go along with this beautiful jaw-dropping scenery, then what are we even doing?"

Schooner *Stephen Taber*'s Stuffed Fried Squash Blossoms

SERVES 4

As a special treat on early summer sails, Captain Noah will step in as guest chef and fry these tiny delicacies on the main deck over a propane burner before the evening meal comes up from the galley. The fillings may vary from trip to trip: veal and ricotta one evening, herbed mascarpone on another. Chef Anna Miller insists they're just as delicious with no stuffing at all. Keep in mind that you will find squash blossoms only at the farmers' market or in your own garden; they are far too delicate and fleeting to appear in any grocery store.

12 fresh blossoms from zucchini (or any other summer or winter squash)

8 ounces ricotta

1 cup all-purpose flour

1 cup lager

1 teaspoon seasoned salt

Canola oil, for frying

1. Carefully inspect the blossoms for lingering insects and snap off stamens and pistils.

2. Fit a disposable pastry bag with a large tip and load it with the ricotta. Placing the tip inside the blossom, squeeze until the petals balloon out with the soft cheese but you are still able to twist the flower shut from the top, safely encasing the cheese inside the flower.

3. Whisk together the flour, beer, and seasoned salt until you have a smooth, thick batter.

4. Pour about 1 inch to 1½ inches of canola oil into a deep, cast-iron skillet and place over a medium-high flame until the oil reaches 375°F.

5. Dip the stuffed blossoms into the batter and then gently lay them in the hot oil.

6. Fry, turning once, until the blossoms are crispy and perfectly golden brown, about 5 minutes.

7. Remove them to a bed of paper towels to drain. Cool slightly before serving.

FROM THE FIELD 59

Carrot and Zucchini Fritters with Yogurt Dipping Sauce

SERVES 8

The recipe for these latke-like fritters, made with summer zucchini and carrots, can be used as a jumping-off point for garden-fresh fritters made from a variety of vegetables. Once you've mastered the technique of getting the excess water out of the vegetables, you could try it with beets, eggplants, parsnips, sweet potatoes, or winter squashes. Let the season's farmers' markets be your inspiration!

Fritters

2 medium zucchini, grated

2 medium carrots, peeled and grated

1 teaspoon sea salt

1 egg, beaten

¼ cup Parmesan cheese

⅓ cup white whole wheat flour

½ teaspoon baking powder

⅓ cup vegetable oil, more if needed

Yogurt Dipping Sauce

½ cup Greek-style yogurt

1 tablespoon mayonnaise

1 teaspoon lemon juice

1 teaspoon Dijon mustard

½ teaspoon honey

¼ teaspoon sea salt

Freshly ground black pepper, to taste

1. In a colander, toss the grated zucchini and carrots with ½ teaspoon of the sea salt. Let sit for 10 minutes.

2. While the vegetables are draining, make the dipping sauce. Whisk together the yogurt, mayonnaise, lemon juice, Dijon mustard, and honey in a small bowl. Add the sea salt and a few grinds of black pepper to taste. Set aside.

3. Press on the grated vegetables with the back of a wooden spoon, squeezing out at as much water as you can. Next, wrap the vegetables in a clean, absorbent dish towel and wring the towel to remove the rest of the water. Taking these steps will ensure a crispy fritter.

4. Add the egg and Parmesan cheese to the zucchini-carrot mixture.

5. Whisk the flour and baking powder together in a small bowl, then add it to the vegetable mixture. Add the remaining ½ teaspoon of sea salt and mix until all the ingredients are combined.

6. Form 8 medium-sized patties by hand, using ¼ cup of the mixture per patty. Heat the vegetable oil over medium-low heat in a cast-iron skillet until a bit of the fritter batter floats and sizzles when dropped in the pan. Working in batches, fry the patties in the oil for 3 to 4 minutes per side, or until golden brown. Remove the fritters to a sheet pan lined with paper towels.

7. Serve the fritters individually or family style, with the dipping sauce alongside.

THE LOST KITCHEN

FREEDOM

Awash in the muted sunlight of early fall, the dining room of the restaurant The Lost Kitchen, located in an 1834 renovated grist mill in Freedom, glows with the burnished gleam of long-used rough-hewn wood. A single bookshelf of cookbooks stands at one end of the large room and a spotless white-tiled open kitchen exudes a timeless fusion of Euro-chic and American homestead. In daylight, the space rests in solitary, unadorned beauty, but by evening, the room will be fragrant with vases of homegrown and locally farmed flowers, the kitchen counters heaped with fresh produce from nearby farms, and the ovens heating cast-iron skillets for the night's dinner service.

The Lost Kitchen's chef-owner, Erin French, who built her unconventional business model largely by intuition, never imagined her restaurant would become the most sought-after reservation in the country.

The Mill at Freedom Falls in Erin's hometown of Freedom is the fourth incarnation of The Lost Kitchen: a unique, hard-won business model that began as a traveling series of secret "supper clubs" and that eventually evolved into a brick-and-mortar restaurant operated in Belfast with Erin and her husband. After the restaurant dissolved—along with Erin's marriage—she took to the road in a vintage Airstream trailer, hosting farm dinners across the state. It was during this time that she pitched the idea for a newly realized Lost Kitchen to the owners of the recently renovated grist mill in Freedom. The restaurant would be seasonal, operating only during the growing season in Maine (a short seed-to-harvest window of about six months) so that the meals could

showcase the region's bounty and best utilize Erin's simple, fresh culinary style.

"I feel embarrassed to say that I'm this awesome cook because it's really not me. It's really the ingredients," Erin insists. "I could not pull off what I pull off if we didn't have farmers doing what they're doing."

It helps, of course, that most of the Lost Kitchen's employees are the very farmers from whom Erin buys her ingredients. As a result, the farmers have a better idea of what stage Erin prefers the produce she uses—herbs that have flowered and bolted, beets and radishes the size and color of jewels.

Erin meets with her "core group" of farmers in February to help plan the coming season's potential menus. They discuss crops that will be specifically grown for the restaurant and seedlings get started shortly thereafter.

The 50-seat restaurant receives over 10,000 reservation requests each spring, all by mail. For a week in April, postcards come from all over the world and Erin and her team pick the season's diners by lottery.

Erin reasons that the restaurant's fame "won't last forever," but that while they enjoy their moment, she and her team are committed to giving their guests the best of Maine in bounty and hospitality—which is a big part of why the restaurant only operates during the height of the growing season. "Because if you only get to eat here once," Erin explains. "I want to give you luscious."

Diners will linger over a four-hour prix-fixe

meal unknown to them until their arrival at the restaurant. In fact, Erin herself often doesn't know the menu until the day's harvests arrive at the restaurant. But she believes that "things that are in season together are designed to go together," and so the night's menu comes together naturally and intuitively.

"It's hard work," she says. "It's physical, it's emotional, it's mental." And it's all a part of a magic formula that Erin attributes to close relationships with local growers and a team who cares as much as she does. And all of it—the ingredients, the mill, the flowers, the open-hearted service—seems to resonate with their dinner guests.

"There's a lot of love here," she says. "It's not just food. It's not just a restaurant. It's a second living room. For all of us."

Erin French's Fried Green Tomatoes with Buttermilk & Chives

SERVES 6

Erin and her team start planning crops for use at the restaurant in late winter. It's months before the first highly anticipated tomato harvest, but Erin says that "the greatest joy is watching someone's smile when they bite into that tomato, and you're like, 'Oh my god, that was six months of work right there.' It's all worth it just for that smile." This recipe for green tomatoes is Erin's go-to when there are tomatoes on the vine, but she just can't wait a second longer for them to ripen. Alternatively, these are a great use of unripe tomatoes brought indoors just before the first frost hits.

Vegetable oil, for frying

Buttermilk Dressing

¼ cup mayonnaise, homemade or store-bought

¼ cup sour cream

2 tablespoons buttermilk

1 tablespoon chopped fresh dill

Salt and pepper

Fried Green Tomatoes

4 green tomatoes

2 cups buttermilk

Salt and pepper

1 cup all-purpose flour

1 cup semolina flour

2 tablespoons chopped fresh dill

Gem marigolds, for garnish (optional)

1. Heat oil in a deep fryer to 375°F or, alternatively, heat 2 inches of oil in a heavy-bottomed pan to the same temperature.

2. In a small bowl, make the buttermilk dressing by whisking together the mayo, sour cream, buttermilk, and dill. Season (liberally) with salt and pepper to taste.

3. Slice the tomatoes into ¼-inch-thick rounds. Put them in a medium bowl with the buttermilk and a pinch each of salt and pepper.

4. In a separate bowl, stir together the flour and semolina. Dredge the tomato rounds in the flour mixture to thoroughly coat. Drop them into the oil 4 to 6 at a time. Do not overcrowd the oil or the temperature will drop and the coating will get soggy. Fry, turning as needed, until the tomatoes are golden brown, 3 to 4 minutes.

5. Remove the tomatoes with a slotted spoon and transfer to paper towels to blot any excess grease. Sprinkle with the chopped dill and drizzle with the buttermilk dressing. Garnish with the edible flowers, if desired.

Erin French's Spring Bread Salad with Asparagus, Radishes, Peas & Mint

SERVES 6

This salad, Erin's riff on a traditional Tuscan dish, showcases The Lost Kitchen's in-the-moment culinary aesthetic that the restaurant is famous for. A riot of spring colors, textures, and flavors—as if a June garden were brought indoors and manicured for the plate—are brought together with a tangy shallot vinaigrette and good bread that has been crisped with olive oil in a hot skillet.

Macerated Shallot Vinaigrette

1 shallot, finely diced

2 tablespoons seasoned rice wine vinegar, or enough to just cover the shallots

¼ cup olive oil

A couple twists of pepper

Salad

1 pound asparagus

3 tablespoons olive oil

Salt and pepper

1 cup shelled fresh peas, blanched

2 bunches mixed radishes, such as French breakfast or any other beautiful radishes that catch your eye, halved

3 cups torn bread

2 tablespoons chopped fresh mint

2 cups pea tendrils or pea shoots

Fresh chives, for serving

1. Preheat the oven to 425°F.

2. To make the vinaigrette, combine the diced shallot and rice vinegar. Allow the combination to macerate for at least 20 minutes or overnight.

3. Whisk in the olive oil and pepper. You only need 2 tablespoons of this dressing for the recipe. You could store the remainder in your fridge for up to a week, but you'll get the freshest, brightest flavor if you use it within 24 hours.

4. To make the salad, cut the asparagus into 2-inch pieces, discarding the tough ends.

5. Arrange the pieces in a single layer on a baking sheet, drizzle with 1 tablespoon of the olive oil, and season with salt and pepper. Give the pan a shake to coat the asparagus. Roast until the pieces are tender but still a bit crunchy, about 5 minutes. Set aside to cool to room temperature.

6. Combine the asparagus, peas, and radishes in a medium bowl. Heat a medium skillet, preferably cast-iron, over medium-high heat, then pour in the remaining 2 tablespoons of olive oil. When the oil shimmers, add the bread and cook, turning partway through, until browned, about 4 minutes. Add to the vegetable mixture. Sprinkle in the mint, pea tendrils, and vinaigrette and toss to dress. Season with more salt and pepper if desired and garnish with a flurry of chives, snipped with kitchen shears.

BEECH HILL FARM

MOUNT DESERT ISLAND

Located on Mount Desert Island, Beech Hill Farm is a six-acre MOFGA-certified organic farm founded in 1989 by Barbarina and Aaron Heyerdahl, both graduates of College of the Atlantic (COA). Barbarina created the original plan for the farm in 1988 as a graduation requirement for her degree in Human Ecology—the only degree offered at the school, which explores the relationships between humans and their natural, social, and built environments.

After running the farm for 10 years, the Heyerdahls donated it to the college in 1999 and granted a conservation easement on the property to Maine Coast Heritage Trust. For 20 years, the farm has served as a hands-on educational resource for students, farmers, and community

members, and provides produce for the college dining hall, a seasonal farm stand, and a student-run food access program serving low-income community members in Bar Harbor.

Of the many benefits that come with a farm managed by a well-endowed educational institution, funding for food access programs like Share the Harvest is a big one. The program works to

fill critical gaps in food access on MDI and generate conversations and actions to address the root causes of food insecurity. Student participants work closely with food pantries to distribute farm stand vouchers, subsidized farm shares, and deliver fresh produce directly to the homes of community members in need.

The college-owned farm also provides a safe place to experiment with new agricultural practices, which could benefit the state's farm communities as a whole. "We have access to a grants writer from COA," farm manager Anna Davis explains. "We've applied for funding for experiments in till practices and field preparation." Normally, this kind of experimentation would be risky for a small family farm barely making ends meet. But for Beech Hill, it's less so. "If it doesn't work, we're not going to go under," Anna explains. Part of the farm managers' jobs at Beech Hill is to record and share the results of their experimentation.

Anna also cites healthcare, a salary that isn't dependent on farm production, and lower stress levels in general among the benefits of farming at Beech Hill. The staff have been able to build and operate a farm stand, which not only sells their own produce, but serves as a retail outlet for dozens of other area farms, food producers, and craftspeople. The farm also secured grants to build a commercial kitchen with the goal of creating a value-added food product inventory that will increase the use of surplus produce. Current products include hot sauces, prepared meals, and packaged frozen vegetables. Anna says that a canned food preservation program is in the works.

Grilled Tomatoes with Herbs on Garlic Toast

SERVES 4

Tomato season is fast and furious in Maine, producing dozens of heirloom varieties that descend upon market stalls in an avalanche of colors, shapes, and sizes. Even cooked on a grill, the tomatoes for this light dish can—and should!—showcase the many motley varieties available from local growers: from candy-sweet Sun Golds and spicy Brandywines to torpedo-shaped Green Tigers and petite Yellow Pears.

Grilled Tomatoes

2 pounds fresh plum-sized tomatoes, halved

2 tablespoons olive oil

1½ tablespoons balsamic vinegar

1 tablespoon chopped fresh oregano

1 tablespoon chopped fresh thyme

1 tablespoon chopped fresh rosemary

Coarse sea salt, to taste

Freshly ground black pepper, to taste

Garlic Toast

½ cup unsalted butter, at room temperature

2 cloves garlic, pushed through a press

1 tablespoon chopped fresh parsley

1 baguette, cut in half lengthwise

¼ cup freshly grated Parmesan cheese

1. Heat a gas grill fitted with a wood chip tray or smoker box on high.

2. Place the cut tomatoes in a large bowl. In a separate bowl, whisk together the olive oil, balsamic vinegar, herbs, salt, and pepper. Drizzle the dressing over the tomatoes, gently tossing them to coat evenly.

3. Place the tomatoes cut side up on a baking sheet lined with foil, and place the baking sheet on the grill grates. Close the cover and roast the tomatoes for 20 to 30 minutes. They should be very soft and starting to char.

4. Place the tomatoes back in the large bowl and cool.

5. To make the garlic toast, mix the butter, garlic, and parsley together in a small bowl. Spread mixture evenly over the baguette halves. Place the bread, cut side down, directly onto the grill grates, and cook until it is toasted and beginning to char.

6. Turn the bread and sprinkle the cut halves with the Parmesan cheese. Cook, covered, for another 2 to 3 minutes, or until the bread begins to turn golden brown and the cheese begins to bubble. Watch the bread carefully to prevent burning. Remove the bread to a cutting board and cut each half into 2 pieces.

7. Spoon the soft, grilled tomatoes onto the baguettes, season with salt and pepper if desired, and serve immediately.

Cream of Tomato Soup

SERVES 4

Make this soup at the height of tomato season, which, in Maine, is late July through mid-September. Everything about this soup highlights the fresh, clean flavor of the tomatoes and passing it through a sieve gives it a luxurious, satiny texture. On a sultry night, you might even consider serving this soup chilled: a smooth take on a summer gazpacho.

2 tablespoons unsalted butter

1 medium yellow onion, chopped

**1 clove garlic, left whole but crushed
    with the side of a knife**

1 teaspoon fennel seeds, crushed (or chopped)

1 tablespoon tomato paste

**2¼ pounds fresh tomatoes, cored
    and roughly chopped**

2 teaspoons granulated sugar

1 bay leaf

2½ cups vegetable stock

¼ cup heavy cream

Sea salt, to taste

Ground black pepper, to taste

1. In a large saucepan, heat the butter until bubbling. Add the onion and garlic clove and sauté gently until softened but not browned. Stir in the crushed fennel seeds and cook for 1 minute. Add the tomato paste and cook for another 2 minutes.

2. Add the chopped tomatoes, sugar, bay leaf, and stock. Bring to a boil, then simmer for 20 minutes. Remove the pan from the heat and cool slightly.

3. Remove the bay leaf from the soup, then transfer the soup in batches to a blender or food processor and blend until smooth. Push the soup through a sieve to remove any skin or seeds, and then return the liquid to the saucepan.

4. Stir in the heavy cream and season to taste with salt and pepper. Reheat gently (but don't boil). When hot, serve immediately.

Creamy Leek and Potato Soup with Olive Oil and Fresh Chives

SERVES 4

Slender leeks, milder in flavor than their bulbous onion cousins, are a natural partner for potatoes, lightening the tuber's deep earthiness with their pleasant herby tang. Leeks are best cooked slowly, in plenty of liquid for a meltingly silky texture in soups and sauces. For this recipe, search out leeks with long, tender whites and crisp green tops. These can be found in the spring markets and have the added benefit of being easy to clean.

2 tablespoons unsalted butter

3 leeks, white parts only, sliced into rings

1 onion, sliced

Pinch of sea salt

2 pounds yellow- or white-fleshed
    potatoes, peeled and thinly sliced

½ teaspoon dried thyme

½ teaspoon dried marjoram

1 bay leaf

5 cups chicken stock

Freshly ground black pepper, to taste

½ cup heavy cream

3 to 4 tablespoons chopped chives

Extra virgin olive oil

Sourdough bread, for serving

1. Melt the butter in a medium-sized soup pot or Dutch oven over a medium heat. When the butter is hot and the foam has subsided, add the leeks, onion, and a pinch of sea salt. Cover the pot with a lid and cook over low heat for 10 minutes.

2. Stir in the potatoes, dried herbs, bay leaf, and another pinch of salt. Cover and cook for 12 minutes, stirring once or twice.

3. Stir in the stock, bring to a boil, and then partially cover the pot and simmer for 30 minutes. Stir the soup from time to time.

4. When everything is soft and falling apart, remove bay leaf and purée the soup with an immersion blender. Alternatively, you can use a blender, but work in small batches to prevent spraying your kitchen with boiling hot soup.

5. Return the soup to a simmer and season to taste with salt and pepper. Just before serving, remove the soup from the heat and stir in the cream.

6. Ladle the soup into serving bowls and garnish with chopped chives and a drizzle of olive oil. Serve each bowl with a hunk of fresh sourdough bread for dipping.

Corn Soup with Parsley

SERVES 4

When summer corn starts appearing in the market stalls and grocery stores in Maine, I commit myself to enjoying it as much as possible in as many ways as possible. I could, of course, eat fresh, boiled corn on the cob slathered in butter every day of the week in July and August, but a recipe like this one—a creamy soup with a pleasant, tender texture—makes sure the other summer vegetables don't get upstaged. A darkly verdant, leafy flat-leaf parsley is a must here, as it is not just a garnish, but balances out the soup's creamy sweetness with its uniquely grassy tang.

3 tablespoons olive oil

1 fennel bulb, diced

2 cloves garlic, finely chopped

Kosher salt

1 Russet potato, peeled and finely diced

4½ cups vegetable broth

½ cup heavy cream

1½ cups (about 3 ears) fresh corn kernels

Freshly ground black pepper

1 tablespoon fresh lemon juice

1 cup fresh flat-leaf parsley, torn

1. Heat the oil in a large saucepan set over medium heat. Add the fennel, garlic, and a pinch of salt, sweating until softened, about 6 to 8 minutes.

2. Stir in the potato and continue to cook for 5 minutes, stirring occasionally. Stir in the broth, cream, corn, and another pinch of salt and pepper.

3. Bring to a boil and then reduce to a simmer until the potato and corn are tender to the tip of a knife, about 20 minutes. Stir in the lemon juice.

4. When ready, season to taste with some more salt and pepper. Ladle into bowls and garnish with the parsley.

NEW ROOTS COOPERATIVE FARM

LEWISTON

New Roots Cooperative Farm is a 30-acre market vegetable farm in Lewiston founded in 2016 by Seynab Ali, Batula Ismail, Jabril Abdi, and Mohamed Abukar—all originally from Somalia. They are graduates of the Cultivating Community's New American Sustainable Agriculture Project and for 10 years farmed at the organization's Packard-Littlefield Farm in Lisbon. The four farmers secured funding and support from Cultivating Community, Cooperative Development Institute, Maine Farmland Trust, Land for Good, and the USDA for the opportunity to farm their own land.

The farm sells their produce through CSA memberships, wholesale accounts, and at six farmers' markets in Lewiston and Southern Maine. They grow close to 50 crops such as amaranth, African varieties of corn and squash, and molokhia. Some of these are new to Maine markets, but are reminiscent of the foods from their home country. The farm cooperative also partners with Isuken Co-op, a food truck owned and operated by members of the Somali Bantu community, which serves a menu of Somali sambusas, stews, injera, and salads.

Sweet Potato and Turnip Soup with Fresh Turmeric

SERVES 4

Because of changing weather patterns, farmers have been able to experiment with crops that aren't historically grown in Maine, such as sweet potatoes. These days, sweet potatoes and rhizomes like turmeric root, are popping up on more and more fall vegetable crop rotations throughout the state. Here, they're paired uniquely in a smooth soup with one of the heartiest of the traditional Maine crops: the turnip.

3 tablespoons olive oil

1 yellow onion, chopped

2 cloves garlic, finely chopped

Sea salt

3 large sweet potatoes, peeled and cubed

1 medium turnip, peeled and cubed

1 cup crimini mushrooms, cleaned and sliced

1 small knob fresh turmeric root (about an inch in length), peeled and finely grated (see Tip)

1½ teaspoons ground paprika

½ teaspoon ground cumin

5 cups vegetable broth

⅔ cup coconut milk, plus extra for serving

1 large handful fresh basil leaves

Freshly ground black pepper, to taste

1 handful fresh flat-leaf parsley, chopped

1. Heat 2 tablespoons of the olive oil in a large saucepan set over low heat. Add the onion, garlic, and a pinch of sea salt. Stir, cover the pan, and sweat the vegetables for 5 to 6 minutes until softened.

2. Stir in the sweet potatoes, turnip, and mushrooms, and sauté over medium heat for 7 to 8 minutes, or until tender to the tip of a knife.

3. Remove about one-quarter of the sweet potato, turnip, and mushroom mixture from the saucepan and set aside until needed.

4. Stir in the turmeric root, paprika, and cumin, and cook for another minute. Pour in the broth and stir well.

5. Bring the soup to a simmer and cook over low heat for about 20 to 25 minutes, or until the sweet potato and turnip are soft enough to blend.

6. When ready, stir in the coconut milk and purée the soup with an immersion blender until smooth. Alternatively, you can puree the soup in batches using a blender.

7. Return the soup to a simmer and season to taste with salt and pepper. Cover and keep warm.

8. When you're ready to serve the soup, heat the remaining 1 tablespoon olive oil in a sauté pan set over medium heat. Add the reserved chopped sweet potato, turnip, and mushroom mixture to the pan and sauté for 2 to 3 minutes, or until fully cooked through and beginning to brown.

9. Ladle the soup into warm bowls. Garnish with the sautéed vegetables, basil leaves, and a sprinkle of chopped parsley before serving.

Tip: If you can't find fresh turmeric, substitute ½ teaspoon ground turmeric.

Young Carrots with Lemon, Thyme, and Olive Oil

SERVES 4

Four Season Farm is famous for their sweet, young "candy carrots." These carrots are about 4 to 6 inches in length and their uniformly narrow shape makes even cooking a breeze.

2 pounds young carrots, peeled

¼ cup olive oil

2 tablespoons honey

1 tablespoon lemon juice

¼ cup chopped fresh thyme

Kosher salt, to taste

Freshly ground black pepper, to taste

1. Preheat the oven to 375°F.

2. Toss the carrots with the olive oil, honey, lemon juice, thyme, and plenty of salt and pepper to taste in a roasting pan.

3. Roast until just tender to the tip of a knife, basting once or twice with juices from the pan, about 40 to 50 minutes.

4. Remove from the oven and serve straight away.

Spinach with Toasted Garlic

SERVES 6

Make this with large leaves of lush, adult spinach (save the baby stuff for delicate salads). Growers like Four Season Farm have spinach available year-round, thanks to the use of greenhouses.

¼ cup unsalted butter

2 tablespoons olive oil

8 cloves garlic, thinly sliced

1 shallot, thinly sliced into rings

12 cups fresh spinach leaves (about
    1¼ pounds), well-rinsed

¼ cup minced red bell pepper

1. Melt the butter with the olive oil in a very large skillet over medium heat until the foam subsides. Add the sliced garlic and shallot and cook, stirring constantly for about 2 minutes, until the garlic is just beginning to brown. Be careful not to let the garlic burn, as it will taint the entire dish with bitterness.

2. Add the spinach leaves and cook for about 4 minutes while tossing with tongs. When all the spinach has wilted, transfer everything to a serving dish and sprinkle with the minced bell pepper. Serve immediately.

WOOD PRAIRIE FAMILY FARM

BRIDGEWATER

In 1940, Maine ranked first in the country for potato yield. In 2019, it ranked tenth. The dozens of potato farms that existed on Route 27 between Presque Isle and Ashland have dwindled to single digits. As the potato industry took off in other states, profitability was only possible for larger farms and many smaller farms converted acreage over to other crops. However, Maine still has most of its farmed acres in potatoes, and 90 percent of those acres are in Aroostook County.

The Gerritsen family at Wood Prairie Family Farm has been growing MOFGA-certified organic potatoes since 1982, supplying organic seed potatoes to farmers and gardeners in Maine and beyond, and providing lots of advice on how to grow and eat them. The farm's acreage is considered moderate, and they grow other market crops for fresh markets and seed. But potatoes are clearly the farm's focus, producing popular varieties such as Yukon Gold and Adirondack Blue, as well as little-known varieties with names like Prairie Blush, Red Cloud, and Rose Finn Apple.

The farm offers a free seed catalog, as well as extensive web-published guides on growing potatoes and potato varieties according to texture. Their e-commerce website offers both seed and ready-to-eat kitchen potatoes for sale, including a popular Maine Organic Potato Sampler of the Month, which ships September through April. Each monthly eight-pound box includes postcard descriptions of each variety of potato, as well as the farm's potato recipe booklet.

FOUR SEASON FARM

BROOKSVILLE

A small hand-painted sign in Harborside quietly marks the location of Four Season Farm, an experimental market garden concept formulated by renowned gardener Eliot Coleman, which took root in 1968 on land previously owned by homesteaders Helen and Scott Nearing. Given the fame of the farm's origins and the notoriety of owner-operators Eliot and his wife, gardener and writer Barbara Damrosch, one might expect a little more hoopla. Instead, the unassuming entrance, at the end of a long, dusty drive over Cape Rosier's serpentine dirt roads, is easy to miss.

But once on the property, a verdant agricultural scene materializes. The farm grows a wide variety of market vegetables on just 2 acres of gently undulating land: a tightly contained patchwork of colors and textures that looks as if it were transported directly from a Tuscan hillside. Using Eliot's highly developed organic practices, which focus on building soil and plant health with farm-based compost and species diversity, the farm's yields exceed what might normally be expected for just 2 acres of production.

The farm provides a reliable year-round supply of produce to markets and restaurants within 40 miles. Growing continues through the winter in eight unheated greenhouses, where plants are grown in well-maintained soil. Customers include Aragosta Restaurant on Deer Isle (page 148), Arborvine Restaurant in Blue Hill, Tinder Hearth in Brooksville, and the Blue Hill Co-op.

Four Season Farm operates a seasonal stand

on the farm itself, which is open one day a week May through September. They also vend at the Winter Market in Blue Hill and are able to offer much of the same produce there as they do in the summer months.

Eliot's daughter, Clara Coleman, a farmer, public speaker, consultant, and writer, took on management of the farm in 2016. While this includes the regular duties of a farm manager such as crop planning, hiring, distribution, and program development, Clara is also using her considerable skills with an eye toward insuring the farm's future. This includes supporting her father's educational legacy by creating tools,

such as videos, to make Eliot's teachings and techniques easily accessible to a new generation of farmers.

Holding true to its founder's philosophy that "Information is like compost; it does no good unless you spread it around," Four Season Farm has a year-round open visitor policy. And while there may not always be someone around who has the time to answer questions, if visitors arrive when the farm stand is open, there's usually an extra hand around, as well as a group of long-time customers and neighbors who seem happy to answer questions about the farm and their gardening practices.

MAINE ORGANIC FARMERS AND GARDENERS ASSOCIATION

UNITY

MOFGA was formed in 1971, a direct result of a catalytic meeting organized by Maine Cooperative Extension educator Charles Gould, and where Helen and Scott Nearing—famed authors of *The Good Life*—were guest speakers. MOFGA's mission was then, and continues to be, to serve as an organization where members share information and learn from each other.

MOFGA quickly became a guiding force for organic farmers and back-to-the-landers across the state, starting an organic certification program and an apprenticeship program in quick succession. The organization also hosted conferences and spearheaded policy initiatives.

The rapidly growing organization found a permanent home in 1996 on 200 acres in Unity, Maine. In 1998, MOFGA's headquarters and year-round education center opened its doors to the public.

The first organized MOFGA harvest festival, known as the Common Ground Country Fair, took place in Litchfield, Maine, in 1977 and drew 10,000 people. The festival now draws 60,000 people over three days at the MOFGA headquarters and fairgrounds in Unity. The celebration is known for its animal and produce exhibitions, as well as the constantly rotating array of food vendors, who must use organic, locally raised meats, produce, grains, and dairy in their offerings.

Today, MOFGA boasts more than 13,000 members, has a staff of 40, provides organic certification for farms and dairies, organizes year-round educational services throughout the state, and offers journeyperson and apprenticeship programs for people interested in becoming organic farmers.

Potato Wedges with Rosemary

SERVES 4

For extra crispy potatoes, preheat your roasting pan in the hot oven and take the time to dry the potato wedges thoroughly before tossing with the oil. Make sure there is plenty of space between the wedges on the pan. Use two sheet pans if one seems too crowded.

2 pounds Russet potatoes, scrubbed and cut into wedges

¼ cup olive oil

1 teaspoon kosher salt

¼ teaspoon freshly ground black pepper

½ cup fresh rosemary sprigs, roughly chopped, plus extra for garnish

1. Preheat the oven to 400°F. Soak the potato wedges in a large bowl of hot water for 10 minutes.

2. Drain well and spread out on paper towels, blotting dry with more paper towels.

3. Toss the potato wedges with the olive oil, salt, pepper, and rosemary in a large bowl.

4. Spill the potatoes onto a hot roasting pan, and cook until golden-brown and tender to the tip of a knife, turning halfway through, 45 to 60 minutes.

5. Remove from the oven and let cool briefly. Serve with more rosemary as a garnish.

Potato and Mustard Gratin

SERVES 4

The wholegrain mustard in this gratin gives this creamy potato dish a welcome lift. Serve it with roasted meats or a hearty kale salad if you want to keep things vegetarian. A crisp white wine wouldn't go amiss here, either.

2 tablespoons soft butter

1 cup whole milk

1 cup heavy cream

2 cloves garlic, crushed with the side of knife

2 bay leaves

2 pounds Russet potatoes, scrubbed, peeled, and cut into ⅛-inch slices

Sea salt, to taste

Freshly ground black pepper

3 tablespoons wholegrain mustard

1. Heat the oven to 350°F. Grease a 10-inch round enameled baking dish or cast-iron skillet with 1 tablespoon of the butter.

2. Combine the milk, cream, garlic, and bay leaves in a saucepan. Bring to a boil over moderate heat. Remove the pan from the heat and allow to sit while you ready the potatoes.

3. Arrange the potato slices in layers in the baking dish, seasoning in between the layers with plenty of salt and pepper.

4. Strain the cream into a large measuring cup and stir in 2 tablespoons of the mustard and salt and pepper to taste. Slowly pour the mixture over the potatoes.

5. Dot the top with 1 tablespoon butter and 1 tablespoon mustard.

6. Transfer the dish to the hot oven and bake until the potatoes are soft to the tip of a knife and golden-brown on top, about 1 hour.

7. Remove from the oven and let stand for 5 to 10 minutes before serving.

Tip: If the potatoes are soft but not browned, place the dish under the broiler for a few minutes until golden and crispy.

Creamed Pearl Onions with Paprika

SERVES 4

Creamed onions are a staple at any New England Thanksgiving dinner, although most recipes are made with pre-peeled frozen white onions. Once you try making the dish with fresh pearl onions (not just white!), you'll never go back.

1⅓ pounds fresh (not frozen) pearl onions

2 tablespoons butter

2 tablespoons all-purpose flour

⅔ cup chicken broth

⅔ cup heavy cream

½ teaspoon sea salt

1 teaspoon paprika, for garnish

1 tablespoon chopped fresh tarragon, for garnish

1. Bring a large pot of water to a boil over high heat. Add the onions and cook until tender to the tip of a knife, 6 to 7 minutes.

2. Drain well and rinse under cold running water. Peel and set aside.

3. Melt the butter in a saucepan set over medium heat. Whisk in the flour and cook the roux until golden, 1 to 2 minutes.

4. Gradually whisk in the broth and cream. Bring to a boil and cook, stirring frequently, until thickened, 3 to 4 minutes.

5. Remove the pan from the heat and stir in the sea salt and the cooked onions. Spoon into a serving dish and garnish with paprika and chopped tarragon.

Roasted Acorn Squash with Brown Sugar and Butter

SERVES 4

Who doesn't love a pool of caramelized brown sugar and melted butter in their own personal squash bowl? Pick squash about the size of a softball, with deep, forest green skins slashed with an occasional swathe of gold. Sweet and comforting, this squash is meant to be eaten from its shell with a spoon. But if you'd like something a little more family-style you may scoop the soft, roasted squash from its skins, mash it, and bring it to the table in a serving bowl.

2 acorn squash

4 tablespoons cold butter, cubed and divided

½ teaspoon sea salt

4 tablespoons light brown sugar

Freshly ground black pepper

1. Preheat the oven to 375°F.

2. Cut the squash in half with a sharp chef's knife. Scoop out the stringy pulp and seeds and discard them.

3. Place the squash halves on a rimmed baking sheet, cut side facing up. Place 1 cube of butter in each squash half and season with the salt.

4. Roast for 30 minutes. Remove from the oven and sprinkle each squash half with 1 tablespoon brown sugar and a turn of ground black pepper.

5. Return the squash to the oven and roast until it is golden brown and very tender to the tip of a knife, 25 to 35 minutes.

6. Remove them from the oven and let cool briefly before serving.

NĪNA JUNE

ROCKPORT

Sara Jenkins, owner and chef of Nīna June restaurant in Rockport, has the unusual distinction of being both a native Mainer and from far away—far, far away.

Daughter of a foreign correspondent and a food writer, Sara grew up abroad, having spent most of her childhood in Italy. The family split their time between Rome and a tumbledown farmhouse in the village of Teverina, where Sara spent a lot of time hanging out in her neighbors' kitchens. "The village was really, really magical," Sara says. "All of our neighbors were hardcore peasant farm-

ers, operating pretty much outside of a monetary economy."

Sara figures that the underlying philosophy of cooking with fresh, home-grown ingredients must have seeped in. "Because when I came back to America for high school," she explains, "I was horrified at what was presented to me as food."

Sara would go on to build her career in the kitchens of Boston, Tuscany, and New York City restaurants, learning from chefs who were passionate about sourcing ultra-fresh ingredients and who practiced nose-to-tail cookery. She opened the NYC-based Porsena, a casual trattoria focusing on artisanal pastas, in 2010.

In 2016, Sara and her family returned to Maine where she opened Nīna June, a light-filled convivial Mediterranean kitchen overlooking Penobscot Bay. And Sara feels like she has come home.

"Up here, we have so much interaction with the farmers, that [the menus are] more driven by what they're producing," Sara explains. "In really traditional Mediterranean food, it's about finding the best ingredient and not doing anything to it. And that would be my cooking philosophy over and over again."

As a result, Nīna June's menu changes daily, but, along with a handful of appetizers, generally features three handmade pastas, a risotto, a fish, and three meats, which could include locally raised pork, lamb, or rabbit.

But freshly harvested vegetables are the colorful building blocks of every one of Sara's plates, echoing the clean, unadulterated food of her childhood in Italy.

"It's what I know," Sara says. "Because of Italy, sourcing this way has always been a theme in my cooking. Long before it was a 'thing.'"

Sara says she's not so interested in sourcing local or organic for the sake of dogma. "For me, locally produced food, whether it's organic or not, inevitably tastes better. And it's a better cycle of life all around."

Sara Jenkins's Eggplant Parmesan

SERVES 4

Sara has been adapting this ultra-simple recipe for Eggplant Parmesan for years, but says she borrowed the original idea from Chris Bianco of Pizzeria Bianco in Phoenix, Arizona. While Sara says you can substitute Grana Padano for the Parmigiano-Reggiano, she insists that the cheese must be from Italy. Otherwise, Maine farm stands abound with tender-skinned eggplants and multi-colored cherry tomatoes all summer long, making this dish an easy locally sourced weeknight standby.

4 medium-sized eggplant

⅓ cup extra virgin olive oil

2 quarts cherry tomatoes

2 or 3 sprigs of basil

½ cup grated Parmigiano-Reggiano
    (or Grana Padano)

Sea salt, to taste

Freshly ground black pepper, to taste

1. Preheat the oven to 400°F. Cut the eggplant into 1- to 1½-inch cubes.

2. In a 9-inch oven-safe terra cotta roasting dish or enameled cast-iron skillet (something that will hold heat), heat 2 tablespoons of oil until it ripples. Toss the eggplant with the remaining olive oil and spread the cubes in a single layer in the skillet. Nestle the cherry tomatoes in among the cubes. Rip the basil leaves with your hands and scatter them over the vegetables.

3. Sprinkle the grated cheese so that it completely covers the dish. Season with salt and pepper to taste.

4. Bake for 15 to 25 minutes, until the eggplant is browned and quite soft, the cherry tomatoes collapsed, and the cheese a golden crust.

5. You can serve hot out of the oven or cooled to room temperature for an excellent summer meal.

Roasted Squash with Pine Nuts

SERVES 4

Delicata Squash is my preferred squash for this recipe, not only for its pretty (and edible!) skin, but also for its mild flavor. It carries the slightly exotic flavors of the spices and also allows the distinct cedar-like taste of pine nuts to shine. Serve this side dish alongside roasted fowl for a classic autumnal meal with a bit of a twist.

1 butternut or 2 delicata squashes

2 tablespoons olive oil

½ teaspoon ground cumin

½ teaspoon ground coriander

1 pinch granulated sugar

**1 teaspoon chopped fresh thyme leave,
    plus extra sprigs for garnish**

1 teaspoon sea salt

¼ teaspoon freshly ground black pepper

½ cup pine nuts

1. Preheat the oven to 350°F.

2. Wash and dry the squash thoroughly, then cut them in half lengthwise and scoop out the seeds and stringy pulp. Peel the butternut squash (if using delicata, no need to peel) then cut into a ¾-inch dice.

3. In a large bowl, toss the squash with the olive oil, cumin, coriander, sugar, thyme, salt, and pepper. Spread the seasoned squash onto an oiled sheet pan and roast for 40 to 45 minutes, or until golden and tender.

4. While the squash is roasting, place the pine nuts in a dry skillet and toast over medium-low heat, stirring often, until they are fragrant and golden. Remove them from heat.

5. When the squash is done, remove it from the oven and spill it into a serving bowl. Scatter the toasted pine nuts on top and garnish with a couple extra sprigs of fresh thyme.

FORE STREET RESTAURANT

PORTLAND

Chef Sam Hayward of Portland's award-winning Fore Street restaurant has been hailed as "Maine's food hero" with a status in Maine equal to that of Alice Waters in California. But when asked about how he became Maine's champion of farm-to-table cuisine, Sam shrugs it off, laying the credit instead at the boots of the state's four-season farmers and fishermen.

When Sam opened his first restaurant, 22 Lincoln, in 1981, there were only two farms in Maine providing wholesale produce for restaurants and institutions.

At that point, Sam had been cooking for almost 10 years and "truck" farms were the only options he knew for Maine-grown produce. And most of that produce was being transported out of state.

The idea of using hyper local produce grown by small family farms close by came to him—or rather, quite literally, showed up on his back door one day—in the form of farmer Frank Gross from Lisbon Falls.

"It was August," Sam recalls. "And he had these leeks, the whites as long as my forearm. Also, carrots, chervil—real chervil that actually tasted like chervil—five different kinds of basil, green beans, and different varieties of tomatoes."

22 Lincoln became a customer on the spot, and the two men—both, Sam jokes, "recovering musicians"—started the first modern Maine chef-farmer relationship—a relationship that has spanned almost 40 years and several restaurants.

Fore Street—twice named to *Gourmet Magazine*'s Top Fifty Restaurants in the United States, and a finalist for a James Beard Award consecutive years since 2011—purchases virtually all their produce and meats from just a handful of small

family farms—including Frank Gross—who plant market crops that suit the restaurant's seasonally changing menu.

Sam encourages other young farmers—new ones that stream in daily through Fore Street's open front door—to break into new markets in underserved parts of the state. He offers suggestions and introductions, fostering the kinds of connections that he has with his own local suppliers.

Winner of the Chef's Collaborative "Sustainer of the Year" award in 2011, Sam seems to accept his position as Maine's reigning chef-advocate for farmers and harvesters with a clear-headed responsibility and a humbleness for which he has become inadvertently famous. He spends a good deal of his time these days "not cooking," he says, but planning the evening's menus with the

restaurant's chef de cuisine and the restaurant's larger off-site events, including collaborations with charities, such as Full Plates Full Potential, which battle food insecurity in Maine. Sam also served on the Board of Directors of the Maine Organic Farmers and Gardeners Association for almost a decade.

Sam attributes the success of Fore Street to business partner Dana Street's vision for an unintimidating, customer-centric, comfortable place to eat, and downplays his own role in the kitchens as merely something that was natural and necessary and right. Sam's relationship to food and cooking is a deeply personal one, which is exemplified—and fortified—by his relationships to the harvesters he has met in the fields, on the boats, and along the rivers of Maine.

SOUTH PAW FARM

FREEDOM

On a sunny day in late September, you'll likely find Meg Mitchell on her midcoast farm, knee deep in the beet field.

"We're harvesting for Herbal Revolution," Meg explains, referring to a local herbalist who uses the beets in one of her popular tonics. "It's great because she likes the big ones."

Meg has a knack for finding specific markets for her produce, whether it's beets for herbal tonics, shallots for Long Grain restaurant's shallot-chile oil, or the ingredients for Chef Cara Stadler's slaw at her popular Portland dumpling house, Bao Bao.

Meg has the ability, like many innovative farmers in Maine, to recognize an opportunity to add value to their produce—a necessity for farmers who want to cut down on the number of crops they grow, but increase their per-acre profitability.

South Paw Farm currently produces 16 crops on 7 acres, and Meg says she's cutting it back little by little every year.

"When you have that huge diversified operation, harvesting all that every week takes a lot of time," explains Meg, whose goals and values shifted when she gave birth to her daughter Lyra in 2016. "I decided I wanted to run a business that didn't take 80 to 90 hours of my time every week."

Meg Mitchell founded South Paw Farm at the age of 21, in Unity, Maine. There she coaxed a scrubby piece of land into a diversified organic farm and discovered a way of life she truly loved. After she met her husband Ryan in 2015, the couple moved the South Paw Farm name and reputation to 64 acres of long-farmed land in Freedom.

The couple inherited the previous owner's market-side chile-roasting business, and Meg recognized an opportunity to increase profitability of her land's most successful crops—peppers,

tomatoes, and onions—by creating a salsa recipe and having it produced by a local co-packer. The farm currently produces approximately 2,400 pounds of tomatoes and 800 pounds of peppers.

"No tomatoes or peppers go to waste," says Meg.

The couple also recognized the value of producing high-quality storage crops—like onions and shallots—filling a hole in the year-round market driven by Maine's high-end restaurants.

On the future of South Paw Farm, Meg says that she eventually wants to reach a plateau where "we have our niches and things are very secure."

She admits that this wasn't her original vision when she started farming at 21.

"But I'm learning to step back and make sure that what I'm pursuing aligns with my current values," Meg says. "Every year it feels more and more possible. We are getting closer to our goal."

Meg Mitchell's Sweet Onion Pie

MAKES ONE 9-INCH PIE

South Paw Farm operates six greenhouses, one of which is used to cure the season's harvest of onions and shallots. Walk into this greenhouse on a sunny day in late fall, and you'll be bowled over with the intoxicating scent of the fragrant roots drying in the sun.

Meg confesses that she might love these two crops more than any other, and this recipe brings out the best of both.

Pie Dough

1 cup plus 2 tablespoons all-purpose flour

½ teaspoon salt

½ teaspoon granulated sugar

8 tablespoons cold, unsalted butter

2 to 4 tablespoons very cold water

Filling

2 tablespoons unsalted butter

1 large yellow onion, sliced

1 large shallot, sliced

2 cloves garlic, chopped finely

1 teaspoon honey

6 eggs

1 cup milk

Salt and pepper, to taste

½ cup grated cheddar cheese (Meg often uses a mixture of local cheeses—cheddar, gouda, jack—whatever she has on hand)

1. Toss the flour, salt, and sugar together in a wide bowl. With a hand grater, grate cold butter directly into the flour mixture, tossing it in as you go. With cold hands, quickly rub the butter into the flour. Leave some flakes big. Drizzle in the cold water, mixing briskly with a rubber spatula as you go. When the mixture is crumbly, but moist, stop adding water. Empty the contents of the bowl onto an un-floured granite slab or wooden board and finish mixing by smearing and scraping the dough with the heel of your hand and a bench scraper. Press the dough together and roll out immediately on a lightly floured surface. Press into a greased 9-inch pie pan, crimp the edges, and put uncooked crust into the refrigerator to chill.

2. While the crust is chilling, melt 2 tablespoons butter in a 9-inch cast-iron skillet over low heat. Toss in the onion, shallot, and garlic, giving them a stir, and cook very slowly for 30 minutes to 1 hour with the lid on. Stir the alliums occasionally, and when they are very soft and quite brown, stir in the honey. Cook for 5 more minutes, then remove the pan from the heat.

3. Preheat the oven to 400°F.

4. In a bowl, beat the eggs and milk together. Season with salt and pepper to taste.

5. Remove the thoroughly chilled crust from the refrigerator and spread the caramelized alliums evenly over the bottom. Pour in the egg-milk mixture and then sprinkle the grated cheese on top.

6. Bake the pie for 20 minutes at 400°F, then reduce the temperature to 350°F and bake for another 20 minutes. The pie is done when the filling is firm, but still a tiny bit wiggly in the center.

7. Cool the pie completely. It's best served at room temperature.

Honeynut Squash with Bacon Stuffing

SERVES 4

Fall means squash of all types at Maine farmers' markets. Honeynut, which looks like a squat, miniature butternut, has extra sweet, nutty flavor and is almost too cute to eat. Because of this, they make a beautiful presentation at your autumn dinner party.

2 honeynut squashes (or two small butternut squashes), about 1½ pounds each

2 tablespoons pumpkin seed oil (if unavailable, use extra virgin olive oil)

1 teaspoon salt

⅛ teaspoon freshly ground black pepper

1 baking potato

1 large carrot

3 tablespoons butter

½ cup milk

⅛ teaspoon ground nutmeg

7 ounces thick slab bacon

2½ ounces (about ½ cup) chopped walnuts

2 tablespoons chopped fresh parsley, for garnish

1. Preheat the oven to 350°F.

2. Cut the squashes in half lengthwise and scoop out the seeds. Rub the cut sides all over with the pumpkin seed oil, then place the halves with the cut side up on a half-sheet pan lined with parchment paper. Season with salt and ground black pepper and bake for 40 to 50 minutes.

3. While the squashes are roasting, peel and dice the potato and carrot. Bring a medium-size pot of water to a boil, add ½ teaspoon salt, and toss in the diced vegetables. Return to a boil and cook at a steady simmer for 15 to 20 minutes, or until the vegetables are quite soft. Drain the vegetables and let the steam escape. Mash them together with a potato masher. Beat in the butter and milk to make a thick purée, and season with ½ teaspoon salt, ground black pepper, and nutmeg.

4. Chop the bacon into ¼-inch dice and fry over a medium flame in a cast-iron skillet until the fat is rendered and the bacon starts to brown. Add the chopped walnuts and fry for another 5 minutes, or until everything is quite fragrant and toasted.

5. When the squashes are golden and soft, remove them from the oven. Scoop out about 1 cup of the hot squash flesh from the shells to make a slightly larger well in the centers. Add the flesh to the potato-carrot puree and mix until smooth.

6. Arrange the squashes on a large platter and fill their hollows with the well-seasoned purée. Spoon over the bacon-walnut sauté, and drizzle with some of the rendered bacon fat. Scatter with chopped parsley before serving.

FROM THE PASTURE

Take a drive down one of Maine's many quiet country roads in mid-summer, and between the leafy hardwood forests and the great stands of evergreens, you'll encounter swaths of open rolling pastured farmland dotted with grazing cows and sheep, and hemmed with barnyards lively with poultry and pigs. And although you won't see crowded feedlots or huge commercial slaughterhouse facilities, raising livestock is very much alive and well in the state.

Most of Maine's livestock and poultry producers are small, often raising animals alongside fields of potatoes or rows of market vegetables. These kinds of conditions, though common in Maine, are considered a luxury in other parts of the country. Pastured animals not only produce meat that is healthier, but also support sustainable and disease-free farmland.

The Maine-raised trademark on meat and poultry is considered valuable enough that in 2019, Governor Janet Mills made it a law that all meats that carry the seal must be born and raised in Maine. This cut out producers that trucked in feedlot cattle from out of state to be slaughtered and sold as "raised in Maine." The state's small family farms that depend on the premium prices for true Maine-raised meat were losing market share as a result. The law ultimately set the stage to protect the highly regarded Maine farm brand.

QUILL'S END FARM

NORTH PENOBSCOT

The sign on Route 15 in rural Penobscot that marks the entrance to Quill's End Farm announces that their on-site store sells yogurt, milk, cream, eggs, beef, lamb, and pork, and is "open Dawn 'til Dusk." If you happen to be a neighbor, then you also know that this sign isn't just an advertisement for what the farm sells, but also a statement about the farmers that live there and their right to choose a life of self-sufficiency in a modern society.

Homesteaders Heather and Phil Retberg founded Quill's End in 2004 with the intention of producing fresh, hyper local dairy and meat for their family and neighbors, promoting ecological

stewardship, and embracing a way of life that resonated deeply with their values.

The farm produces grass-fed beef and veal, eggs and chickens from pasture-raised poultry, and pork raised in the woods and on pasture. They also process cream, milk, yogurt, and fresh cheeses from cows and goats. They sell their goods through a local buying co-op, a nearby farm drop, and from a postage stamp–sized self-service farm store on their property.

The Retbergs farm full-time, supply 60 families with fresh meat and dairy through their buying clubs, and serve 150 to 200 people a week from their farm store.

But the privilege to live a full-time farming life was hard-won, according to Heather.

Just as the couple had gotten the farm to the point where it could feed their family and allow them to let go of secondary jobs off the farm, the state told them that they could not sell their poultry and dairy products to their neighbors unless they built their own on-site USDA processing facility.

"It would have required us to work another decade off the farm to pay for the facility," Heather recounts. "So our choices were quit or change something. If we did nothing, the outcome was clear; we quit. Everyone quits."

Heather reasoned that the state mandates not only made it impossible for them to farm exclusively for their small community, but also threatened the growth of farming in the state by making it cost prohibitive for new farmers to support themselves while they built a commercial customer base.

The alternative to quitting, of course, was to jump into a charged political fight.

The Retbergs opted for change, and Heather began to lay the groundwork for her town to adopt an ordinance for food sovereignty—a policy that allows municipalities to regulate their own local food systems, including production, processing, consumption, and direct producer-to-consumer exchanges. By 2011, Heather had not only successfully lobbied several municipalities in her region to adopt a "home rule" food ordinance, but had become one of the leading voices for the food sovereignty movement in Maine.

In 2017, after years of garnering local and state support, Maine's food sovereignty law—An Act To Recognize Local Control Regarding Food Systems—was passed. Today, 74 towns in every one of the state's 16 counties have adopted a local food sovereignty ordinance.

Heather says there's still work to do. She's con-

cerned that the law might discourage municipalities from inviting their constituents to participate in the home rule interpretation process. But she admits she's thrilled with how far the state has come in just a few years. "So long as we stay engaged," she says.

Crostini with Chicken Liver and Caramelized Shallots

SERVES 4

Chicken livers are chock full of protein and a great source of vitamin A, vitamin B-12, riboflavin, folate, and iron. However, many people shy away from consuming liver because of the function it performs in living birds—a filter for digestion and waste products. Farms like Quill's End serve an invaluable purpose for community members who depend on knowing how their food was raised, ensuring a transparent, non-toxic food system from start to finish.

4 slices ciabatta (8 slices if the loaf is long and thin)

1 tablespoon olive oil

2 tablespoons butter

4 large shallots, peeled and thinly sliced

1 garlic clove, peeled and finely chopped

1¼ pounds chicken liver, cleaned and cut in a ¼-inch dice

¼ cup dry red wine

1 teaspoon chopped fresh thyme leaves

2 tablespoons balsamic vinegar

Sea salt, to taste

Freshly ground black pepper, to taste

2 tablespoons chopped fresh parsley, for garnish

1. Preheat the oven to 375°F. Brush both sides of the bread slices with olive oil and place on a sheet pan. Toast the slices for 10 to 12 minutes, flipping them halfway through. The bread is done when it is golden brown all over. Remove the pan from the oven and place the toasted bread on a cooling rack.

2. Heat the butter in a large cast-iron skillet over a medium-low flame. Add the shallots and garlic and cook, stirring occasionally, until the alliums are quite soft and deeply browned, 15 to 20 minutes.

3. Increase the heat to moderate, add the chopped liver to the skillet, and cook, stirring, for a few minutes. Deglaze the skillet with the red wine.

4. Reduce the liquid until the mixture is jammy, but not dry, 2 to 3 minutes. Scatter in the thyme and season with the balsamic vinegar, sea salt, and freshly ground black pepper.

5. Cut each slice of crostini in half diagonally and arrange on an appetizer tray. Divide the filling between the 4 (or 8) crostini, scatter with the chopped parsley, and serve.

Chicken Wings with Blueberry Barbecue Sauce

SERVES 4

Spicy, sweet, tangy, and utterly irresistible, these wings are classic game-day food with a distinctly Maine twist. Many farms these days are creating lines of value-added products to use up surplus produce, so finding a locally made barbecue sauce to use as your base in this recipe could be as easy as shopping at your local farmers' market or food co-op.

Blueberry Barbecue Sauce

1 tablespoon olive oil

1 small white onion, finely chopped

1 clove garlic, finely chopped

1 cup fresh or frozen Maine blueberries

½ cup maple syrup

2 cups pre-made barbecue sauce

¼ cup sherry vinegar

1 tablespoon ground chipotle pepper

1 tablespoon ground ancho chile

Wings and Drumsticks

1½ pounds chicken wings and mini drumsticks

Sea salt, to taste

Freshly ground black pepper, to taste

1. To make the Blueberry Barbecue Sauce: Heat the olive oil in a large heavy-bottomed saucepan over medium heat. Sauté the onion and garlic until quite soft and caramelized. Add blueberries, maple syrup, barbecue sauce, sherry vinegar, ground chipotle, and ancho chile, and bring to a boil. Reduce heat to low and simmer the sauce for 15 minutes.

2. To make the wings and drumsticks: Preheat the oven to 400°F. Season chicken with sea salt and black pepper. Spill the chicken pieces out onto an oiled sheet pan and roast for 30 minutes, or until the internal temperature reads 165°F. Remove the pan from the oven and transfer the wings into a large, heat-proof bowl. Add the Blueberry Barbecue Sauce, and toss together so that all the wings are thoroughly coated. Heap the wings onto serving platter, and serve any remaining sauce alongside.

MISTY BROOK FARM

ALBION

As a child, Katia Holmes wanted to be a large animal vet when she grew up. So rather than going straight to college after high school, she went to work on a friend's biodynamic dairy farm.

"I discovered that it was a lot more fun to take care of cows and keep them healthy than running around fixing everyone else's problems," Katia says.

The holistic rotational practices and the focus on natural animal and plant health that make up the foundation of biodynamic farming resonated with Katia, and she and her husband, Brendan Holmes, founded Misty Brook Farm in 2005 with those principles in mind.

Today, the farm is MOFGA-certified organic and managed with what Katia calls a "biodynamic mindset," in the sense that crops and animals move across the farm in a rotation. This practice keeps them free of disease and also prevents soil depletion.

The 600-acre farm raises eggs, poultry, beef, veal, lamb, mutton, and pork. They also produce raw milk and cream, whole grains and self-milled flours, dried beans, raw sheep's milk, and wool. The couple's teenaged son, Alister, also grows a ½ acre of market vegetables for their farm stand at the annual Common Ground Country Fair.

Katia says they don't do weekly farmers' markets anymore and instead have concentrated their sales efforts into a state-wide wholesale mar-

ket and their on-site Farm Store. With three dedicated trucks, they work with other small farms to provide a much-needed delivery service, making it affordable for small farm-produced products to reach a wider market.

Their roadside Farm Store is open 24 hours a day, 365 days a year. Neighbors know how to turn on and off the lights, and an honor-based accounting and payment system seems to work just fine. In the store, freezers and refrigerators are packed with frozen butchered meats, milk, cream, and half-and-half in all-size containers, and eggs. Shelves are lined with whole and milled grains, dried beans, and honey from nearby apiaries.

The farm sells to a few passionate farm-to-table restaurants, including Meridians Kitchen and Bar in Fairfield, Aragosta in Deer Isle, The Brooklin Inn, and the Eat at Joe's food truck in Ellsworth. They also supply Fuzzy Udder Creamery with their surplus sheep's milk.

Katia says they'll continue to grow their production according to the improvement of their soil, but no faster, and no more than the soil can handle.

Misty Brook is one of just a handful of farms in Maine with such a diverse species population—and definitely the largest.

Katia says, "We'd really like to be an example for a way things can be done. In tune with nature and working together."

Sliced Lamb Salad with Tomatoes, Feta, and Red Onions

SERVES 4

Serve this substantial salad for a late-summer luncheon on the deck where you can thoroughly enjoy the aromas of grill-roasted lamb and fresh tomatoes. Maine lamb is full of flavor and tastes very different from the Australian lamb that is readily available year-round in the meat cases of most grocery stores. Many farms, like Misty Brook, have an on-site farm store with freezers full of packaged cuts of meat. For the most part, these stores are run on the honor system—customers let themselves in, pick from an array of products that might include fresh eggs, milled grains, fresh and frozen meats, dairy products, honey, and maple syrup. They record their purchase in a notebook, pay via cash or a check left in a coffee can or money box, and then turn out the lights when they leave.

Lamb

1 pound piece boneless leg of lamb, about 3 inches thick

Olive oil, for rubbing

1 teaspoon ground cumin

½ teaspoon sea salt

½ teaspoon freshly ground black pepper

Dressing

3 tablespoons white wine vinegar

1 teaspoon honey

½ teaspoon dry mustard

½ teaspoon cumin

¼ cup olive oil

Sea salt and white pepper, to taste

Salad

2 cups heirloom cherry tomatoes of varying colors, halved

1 large tomato, cored and sliced

1 large red onion, thinly sliced

1 large thin-skinned cucumber, sliced

½ cup pitted kalamata olives

¾ cup crumbled feta, for garnish

1. Light a grill to 375°F. For charcoal grills, if you can hover your palm over the grill for 3 to 4 seconds, you have reached the correct temperature. Rub the lamb with olive oil, cumin, sea salt, and black pepper. Let the meat stand at room temperature for 10 minutes.

2. While the grill heats up, make the dressing. In a bowl, combine the white wine vinegar, honey, mustard, and cumin. Whisk in ¼ cup olive oil and season with salt and white pepper to taste.

3. Grill the lamb over moderate heat, turning a few times, until charred and medium-rare, 15 to 20 minutes or until the internal temperature reads 125°F. Transfer the lamb to a carving board and let the meat rest for five minutes.

4. In a large bowl, toss the tomatoes, red onion, cucumber, and olives. Add the dressing and toss well. Spread the vegetables on a large serving platter. Thinly slice the lamb against the grain and arrange the slices on top of the vegetables. Garnish the salad with the feta and serve.

Creamy Turkey and Wild Rice Soup

SERVES 4

If you have leftovers from a roast turkey dinner, this is an excellent use for them. Don't feel hemmed into using just the breast meat. The slight gaminess of leg and thigh meat goes perfectly with the somewhat unconventional flavor of the wild rice.

2 cups water

½ cup wild rice

1½ tablespoons butter

1 large shallot, finely chopped

2 carrots, peeled and cut in a ¼-inch dice

1 tablespoon all-purpose flour

½ teaspoon sea salt

¼ teaspoon white pepper

Pinch of sugar

¼ cup dry white wine

2½ cups vegetable stock

1⅔ cups cooked turkey breast,
     cut into a ½-inch dice

¾ cup heavy cream

1. Bring the water to boil over high heat in a medium saucepan. Place the rice in a sieve and rinse thoroughly with cold water. When the water boils, add the rice, reduce the heat to low, cover, and simmer for 30 to 45 minutes, or until the rice is tender and some of the grains have burst. Drain the rice in a mesh sieve, fluff, and set aside.

2. In a medium soup pot over medium heat, melt the butter until it's bubbling and hot. Add the chopped shallot and sauté until it starts to soften, 3 to 5 minutes. Add the carrots and sauté for a few minutes more. Sprinkle in the flour and season with salt, white pepper, and sugar. Add the wine and stir

until smooth. Pour in the stock, cover the pot, and simmer for 5 to 10 minutes.

3. Add the turkey to the pot and simmer for another 5 minutes. Reduce the heat slightly and stir in the cream. Depending on the desired consistency, simmer for a few more minutes to thicken, or add more stock to thin out.

4. Finally, add the rice to the pot. Season with salt and pepper to taste and serve.

PINELAND FARMS

NEW GLOUCESTER

Just outside of Freeport, situated among rolling hills and the pristine white fences of neighboring horse farms is the well-manicured, gracefully sprawling 5,000-acre agricultural resource campus known as Pineland Farms.

True to its name, the center is made up of almost equal parts evergreen forests and open land; the forests are host to more than 16 miles of year-round recreational trails and much of the open land is employed in agricultural pursuits.

Founded in 1908 by the State of Maine, Pineland Farms was originally the home for the Maine School for the Feeble Minded. The facility, which operated under several different names through the decades, and which also included several thousand acres of commercially farmed land, served as a ward and treatment center for mentally disabled patients for close to 90 years.

In 2000, a non-profit bought the land and began transforming Pineland Farms into what it is today—recreational area, educational facility, vegetable farm, equestrian center, marketplace, restaurant, world-class dairy farm, and headquarters for Pineland Farms Natural Meats.

From its humble beginnings as the country's first ever organic/alternative beef operation at neighboring Wolfe's Neck Center for Agriculture & the Environment in Freeport, Pineland's meat division has grown exponentially over the years. Today, the company partners with over 200 small family beef farms to produce natural, hormone- and antibiotic-free beef products.

The on-site dairy produces eight different kinds of cheeses, as well as fresh cheese curds. Milk comes from partner farms, as well as Pineland's own herd of registered Holsteins. The center cultivates 300 acres of market vegetables for both direct sale at their on-site Pineland Farms Market and resale with local retail partners. Their produce, meats, and cheeses make up the menu of fresh salads, sandwiches, take-home dinners, and pastries at the center's Commons Kitchen, which is operated by Portland-based The Black Tie Company.

Country Beef Stew

SERVES 4 TO 6

Rich meat stews play a big role in rural Maine farm kitchens in the fall and winter months. These long-cooked stews have the dual benefit of both warming chilly farmhouses and tenderizing economical cuts of meat such as beef chuck. Although not the most coveted parts of the cow, chuck roasts are often what's left after the more profitable cuts from the loins and ribs have been sold. Chuck and rump roasts have less fat and more connective tissue and, while they require long and moist cooking, they also have more protein and, often, more flavor. Long cooking with sturdy storage vegetables, such as carrots and onions, imbue everything with rich meaty flavor and produce fork-tender morsels that warm you from the inside out.

2½ pounds beef chuck roast, trimmed and cut into 1½-inch dice

Sea salt

Freshly ground black pepper

4 tablespoons all-purpose flour

4 tablespoons sunflower or canola oil

2 tablespoons unsalted butter

1 yellow onion, chopped finely

3 large carrots, peeled and cut into ½-inch dice

2 celery stalks, cut into ½-inch dice

1 large leek, green top discarded, whites halved lengthwise and sliced into half rounds

1½ cups full-bodied red wine, such as Merlot or Cabernet Sauvignon

3 vine tomatoes, cored and roughly chopped

2 bay leaves

3 to 4 thyme sprigs

2 to 3 rosemary sprigs

2½ cups beef broth

1. Preheat the oven to 325°F.

2. Season the meat generously with salt and pepper. Dredge the pieces in flour, shaking off excess.

3. Heat 1 tablespoon of the oil in a cast-iron pot or Dutch oven set over a moderate heat. Working in three batches, brown the chuck roast in hot oil, making sure not to overcrowd the pot, using 1 table-spoon of oil for each batch. Remove the meat to a plate and set aside.

4. Once you've browned all the meat, reduce the heat to medium and add the remaining oil and the butter.

5. Stir in the onion, carrots, celery, leek, and a generous pinch of salt, and sweat the vegetables until softened and starting to color, 7 to 8 minutes.

6. Deglaze the pot with some red wine, scraping to release bits. Return the browned meat to the pot, along with any accumulated juices, and add the tomatoes, bay leaves, and thyme and rosemary sprigs, and stir.

7. Cover everything with the remaining wine and the beef broth. Bring to a boil, cover with an oven-proof lid, and transfer the pot to the oven. Cook until the meat is tender and can be pulled apart between your fingers, 2 to 2½ hours.

8. When ready, remove the pot from the oven and let cool briefly with the lid off. Adjust seasoning to taste with salt and pepper before serving.

Pot Roast

SERVES 6

Top round roasts, another frugal cut of meat, is a great choice for pot roasts and does well with strongly flavored root vegetables like parsnips, turnips, and carrots. The goal here is to produce a tender, sliceable roast that can serve both as a Sunday supper and as a flavorful addition to weekday sandwiches.

2¼ pounds top round beef roast, trimmed and tied

1 teaspoon sea salt

½ teaspoon freshly ground black pepper

⅓ cup olive oil

4 cloves garlic, peeled and crushed

4 large carrots, peeled and cut into ½-inch dice

4 large parsnips, peeled and cut into ½-inch dice

1 baby turnip (about ½ pound), peeled
    and cut into ½-inch dice

1 cup dry white wine

1 small bunch of fresh rosemary

1 cup beef stock

2 tablespoons finely chopped flat-leaf parsley

1. Preheat the oven to 300°F.

2. Rub the meat all over with the salt and pepper.

3. Heat two tablespoons of the olive oil in a large cast-iron pot or Dutch oven over medium heat until hot. Add the meat to the pot and brown it on all sides. Remove the roast from pot.

4. Add the remaining oil to the pot, followed by the garlic, carrots, parsnips, and turnip. Cook the vegetables for 4 to 5 minutes, stirring occasionally, until they start to soften.

5. Deglaze the pot with the white wine, add a sprig of rosemary, and then simmer until the liquid is reduced by half. Add the beef stock, stir well, and position the beef over the vegetables.

6. Transfer the pot to the oven to roast for 2½ hours, or until the beef is tender and registers at least 150°F on a meat thermometer.

7. Remove the pot from the oven, cover it loosely with aluminum foil, and allow the roast to rest for at least 15 minutes.

8. Garnish the roast with the rest of the fresh herbs before serving.

BLUE HILL BLONDES

BLUE HILL

Debussy spills from the cow barn on John and Betty Tyler's property on Tamworth Farm Road in Blue Hill, mingling with the birdsongs of early fall migrators and the gentle rustle of leaves.

"They prefer classical music," Betty says, referring to the small herd of Blonde D'Aquitaine cows in the barn, sheltering convivially from the mid-afternoon sun. "They do better if you treat them better."

And the animals—not your average farm cows—certainly look ridiculously content, their soft champagne-colored coats gleaming in shafts of sunlight.

The herd feeds on grass through three seasons, and winters on hay. Betty admits, however, they really do like apples and once broke through the fences to reach a neighbor's fruiting tree.

While the Tylers are friendly enough with the herd that they call each cow by name, play their favorite music, and allow an entire acre of grass for each of them, they also know the endgame. Their freezer is stocked with flash frozen cuts from last fall's slaughter, available for customers that drop by the farm, and at the Blue Hill Farmers' Market on Saturdays. D'Aquitaine meat has virtually no fat, but is so tender that you'd never notice. Blue Hill Blonde beef is also featured on the menus of high-end restaurants in the area, including Aragosta, The Brooklin Inn, and Arborvine.

Blue Hill Blondes Oven-Baked Short Ribs

SERVES 4

Tender beef short ribs are a crowd-pleaser any time of year, but especially welcome in the early fall months when we're not quite ready to light the woodstove, but welcome the extra heat from a warm oven and the savory aroma of a brandy-spiked meal.

¼ cup unsalted butter

¼ pound salt pork, diced

4 pounds beef short ribs, cut into serving-size pieces

One 10-ounce can Campbell's Condensed Golden Mushroom Soup

½ cup water

¼ cup brandy

2 tablespoons fresh lemon juice

1. Preheat the oven to 400°F.

2. Melt the butter in an enameled soup pot or Dutch oven over medium heat. Add the salt pork and cook until the fat is rendered.

3. Add the short ribs and brown on all sides. If necessary, work in batches, setting aside browned ribs to make room for the next batch; this will prevent overcrowding the pan, which will hinder browning.

4. In a small bowl, stir together the soup, water, and brandy. Return all the ribs to the pot, and then pour over the soup mixture. Simmer for 10 minutes.

5. Cover the pot and transfer to the oven. Bake for 30 minutes. Reduce the heat to 350°F, and bake for an hour more.

6. When the ribs are cooked through and the meat is falling off the bone, remove the pot from the oven, add the lemon juice, and serve immediately.

Filet Mignon with Peppered Pears

SERVES 4

Make this pretty, autumnal dish for an unhurried dinner party where your guests can take their time appreciating how all the flavors and textures come together. Choose ripe but firm pears that will hold up to poaching. Doing so will ensure that the pears absorb the flavors of the wine, honey, and peppercorns without first turning to mush. Small-sized varieties such as Seckel are suited in size to petite filets and look very attractive in the finished dish.

2 ripe pears

2½ cups white wine

3 tablespoons honey

1 tablespoon whole peppercorns

2 leeks, white parts only

1 small bunch fresh thyme, reserving
    some sprigs for garnish

2 tablespoons butter

Sea salt

Freshly ground black pepper

2 tablespoons olive oil

4 beef tenderloin steaks, approximately
    6 to 8 ounces each

1. Peel the pears, slice in half lengthwise, and core them.

2. Place the wine, honey, and peppercorns in a pan and bring to a boil. Add the pears, cover, and simmer over medium heat for 15 to 20 minutes. They should be soft, but not falling apart. Drain the pears, reserving about 1 cup of the cooking liquid. Set aside.

3. Slice the leeks into ⅛-inch rounds. De-stem a few sprigs of the thyme and chop the leaves so that you have about 2 teaspoons.

4. Heat the butter in a sauté pan over medium low heat and gently sauté the leeks until almost tender. Add ¾ cup of the pear cooking liquid to the pan, season to taste with salt and pepper, and simmer for 6 minutes, or until the liquid is reduced and slightly syrupy, and the leeks are quite soft. Stir in the chopped thyme leaves.

5. While the leeks are cooking, heat the olive oil over medium-high heat in a large cast-iron skillet. Season the steaks with salt and pepper and cook for 6 to 8 minutes per side for medium-rare (internal temperature should read 130° to 135°F), or until cooked to your liking. Remove the steaks from the skillet and allow them to rest on a cutting board while you prep the plates.

6. Slice each pear half open like a fan. Arrange the leeks in a pool of sauce on warmed dinner plates, place the steaks on top of the leeks, and then place the fanned pear half on top of the steaks. Garnish with freshly ground black pepper and a thyme sprig.

New England Boiled Dinner

SERVES 4

For the uninitiated, a "boiled dinner" doesn't sound like anything good. But this late-winter homestead staple is built for flavor and is best served with crusty bread and lots of good butter. Similar to corned beef and cabbage, boiled dinners are meant to be enjoyed hot and freshly made in late winter, accompanied by a crisp lager and good company.

- 3 pounds corned beef brisket, with spice packet, trimmed of excess fat
- 2 bay leaves
- 3 fresh thyme sprigs, plus extra for serving
- 2 fresh rosemary sprigs
- 4 celery stalks, trimmed and cut into sections
- 3 large carrots, peeled and cut into sections
- 1 pound baby potatoes, or larger potatoes halved or quartered
- 2 tablespoons unsalted butter
- 1 medium green cabbage, quartered or roughly sliced
- Sea salt, to taste
- Freshly ground black pepper, to taste
- A loaf of fresh, crusty French bread, for serving

1. Place the brisket in a large Dutch oven and cover with water. Stir in the spice packet contents, bay leaves, thyme, and rosemary.

2. Bring to a boil over a moderate heat and then reduce to a simmer, cooking until the brisket is tender, about 3 hours; check on the water level every 30 minutes or so, topping up as needed.

3. Stir in the celery, carrots, and potatoes, and continue to cook at a steady simmer until tender, about 20 minutes.

4. In the meantime, melt the butter in a large skillet set over a medium heat. Add the cabbage, a generous splash of water, and a pinch of salt and pepper, covering the skillet with a lid.

5. Cook over a reduced heat until tender, stirring occasionally, 6 to 9 minutes.

6. Remove the brisket from the Dutch oven and let it rest under aluminum foil for 10 minutes before slicing. Reheat the cabbage and vegetables as needed before dividing between plates along with the beef.

7. Garnish with a little chopped thyme and serve with thick slices of crusty bread and a cold beer.

EAT AT JOE'S FOOD TRUCK

ELLSWORTH

A glance at the Eat at Joe's food truck menu at Fogtown Brewing Company in Ellsworth doesn't look much different than your average outdoor hamburger shack. And that seems to be the way proprietor Joe Segari—a retired plumber from New Jersey—likes it. Cheeseburgers, chili burgers, bacon burgers, Reubens, and fries.

But it's what isn't listed on the menu that really defines the food at Eat at Joe's: ketchup made from scratch, homemade salsa, house-cured bacon, corned beef, pastrami, slow-cooked brisket—all crafted by Joe and his wife Nancy with 100 percent of their ingredients sourced from local farms.

"We do it that way because it's the right thing to do," Joe says.

In fact, Joe would rather sing the praises of the farmers and bakers he sources from than showcase his own cooking prowess. The eatery has no website, and its Facebook page highlights live music acts at the brewery and the accomplishments of the area's local farms. Joe feels that he owes the food truck's success to the word-of-mouth advertising he's received from his vendors—and he pays it back in spades.

Six days a week, in the bitter cold of February, and in the lazy humid days of summer, you'll find Joe over the grill, simultaneously flipping burgers and checking his phone for texted orders.

The truck, which operates year round from its permanent spot on the patio of the popular Ellsworth brewpub, supplies the only on-site food for

patrons of the brewery, and is also a local standby for families looking for take-out options that match their values—and their pocketbooks.

"We wanted to make this kind of experience available for people who don't have big money to go to restaurants," Joe says.

Everything on the menu is less than $20 and Joe doesn't skimp on serving size and quality.

Each day, Joe updates a list of daily specials on a sandwich board, highlighting seasonal produce or a special menu item made with Fogtown beer to celebrate a new release from the brewery.

Among the most popular items on the menu are Joe's Reubens—a tall stack of house-cured meat and melty cheese, on a homespun rye from the bread makers at Tinder Hearth in Brooksville. Another board lists the farms customers can choose from for the beef in their burger.

"We don't really make much money," Joe admits, "but I'm proud that we have the ability to source everything we serve from local farms. And I'm really proud of that."

Braised Lamb Shanks with Root Vegetables and Chickpeas

SERVES 4

Sheep production in Maine was once one of the state's most important agricultural industries. During the Civil War, Maine was home to nearly a million head of sheep, as the demand for wool was at its highest. By 1880, the sheep population had declined by half and continued a slow steady decline into the 20th and 21st centuries. Today, Maine's sheep count hovers just around 50,000.

By the numbers, sheepherding in Maine may be an insignificant agricultural pursuit, but it is one steeped in tradition, romance, and history. To this day, there are still sheep farmers that allow their flocks to roam on Maine's few sheep-only islands, visiting only three times per year; in the spring for lambing, in the summer for shearing, and in the fall to bring a portion of the flock to the mainland for meat production.

Sheep farmers in Maine harvest both lambs and mutton, and many prefer the gamier taste of meat from the adult animals.

This dish utilizes an economical cut in a rustic braise. Serve it alongside toothy farro or short-grain brown rice. Shanks have a lot of bone and the meat tends to shrink as it cooks, so definitely plan for one shank per person. Serve the dish with the bone for rustic presentation and best flavor.

4 small lamb shanks

Sea salt

Freshly ground black pepper

2 tablespoons olive oil

2 onions, peeled and roughly chopped

4 carrots, peeled and cut into ½ inch rounds

2 cloves garlic, peeled and chopped

1 celery root, peeled and cut into ½ inch dice

1 tablespoon tomato paste

1 cup red wine

1½ cups beef stock, plus extra as needed

2 sprigs fresh tarragon

4 sprigs fresh thyme

One 14-ounce can chickpeas

1. Preheat the oven to 325°F.

2. Season the lamb shanks with salt and ground black pepper. Heat the olive oil over medium-high heat in a large cast-iron pot or Dutch oven. Working in two batches, add two shanks and brown the meat on all sides. Remove the shanks and set aside, repeating for the remaining shanks.

3. Add onions, carrots, garlic, and celery root to the pot. Stir in the tomato paste and allow vegetables to sweat for 5 to 7 minutes. Deglaze the pot with the red wine and add a splash of stock.

4. Return the lamb shanks to the pot, add the herbs, cover the pot with an oven-proof lid, and place it in the oven. Cook for 2½ hours. Turn lamb shanks frequently during cooking, adding stock as needed. During last 20 minutes of the cooking time, rinse and drain the chickpeas and add them to the pot.

5. Remove the pot from the oven, season to taste, and serve immediately.

Pan-Roasted Lamb Chops with Mint Pesto and Carrot Puree

SERVES 4

As spring meals go, there are few more perfect than young, tender lamb paired with flavorful spring vegetables and herbs. Here, mint pesto—so much better than neon green jelly from a jar!—dresses petite chops and makes a striking contrast with silky carrot puree and sharp spring onions. For a fancy spring fete, purchase lollypop-like rib chops with cleaned bones.

Mint Pesto

½ cup pine nuts

1 large bunch mint, leaves only, washed and dried

½ bunch flat-leaf parsley, leaves only, washed and dried

½ cup (about 2 ounces) Parmesan, grated

⅔ cup olive oil

Sea salt to taste

Freshly ground black pepper

1 to 2 tablespoons freshly squeezed lemon juice

Carrot Puree

3 large carrots, peeled and roughly chopped

1 garlic clove, crushed

⅔ cup vegetable stock

3 tablespoons heavy cream

1 tablespoon unsalted butter

Lamb

8 lamb ribs or loin chops

4 tablespoons olive oil

For Serving

2 tablespoons olive oil

6 spring onions (preferably with small, purple bulbs), roots removed and greens trimmed to 3 inches

Fresh mint leaves

1. To make the mint pesto: Place the pine nuts in a dry frying pan set over a medium heat. Toast until golden and aromatic. Spill them into a food processor.

2. Add the mint leaves, parsley, Parmesan, and half of the olive oil to the food processor. Pulse until the mixture is broken down and coarse.

3. With the food processor on, drizzle in the remaining olive oil until the pesto comes together into a smooth sauce. Scrape the pesto into a bowl and season to taste with salt, pepper, and the lemon juice. Cover the sauce and chill until ready to use.

4. To make the carrot puree: Combine the carrots with the garlic and vegetable stock in a heavy-based saucepan. Bring the vegetables to a simmer, cover, and cook over medium heat until the carrots are tender, 12 to 15 minutes.

5. Remove pan from heat and scrape the vegetables into a clean food processor. Add the cream and butter, and puree until smooth. Season to taste with salt and pepper. Scrape the puree into a bowl, cover, and set aside.

6. To make the lamb: Heat a large, cast-iron skillet over medium heat until hot. While the skillet is heating, rub the lamb chops with olive oil and season with salt and pepper.

7. Cook the chops in the hot pan, turning occasionally, until golden brown all over and firm, yet springy to the touch, 6 to 8 minutes, turning occasionally (if you're using a meat thermometer, shoot for an internal temperature of 125°F for medium-rare).

8. Remove the chops to a plate and cover loosely with aluminum foil, leaving to rest for at least 5 minutes.

9. For serving: Heat the olive oil in a clean cast-iron skillet over medium heat. If the onions are on the large side, split them in half lengthwise. Add them to the pan, season with salt and pepper, and cook until charred all over, 2 to 3 minutes. Remove from heat and set aside.

10. Reheat the carrot puree in a saucepan over a low heat, stirring. Spread onto a large serving plate and top with the chops.

11. Drizzle some of the mint pesto over the plate. Arrange the spring onions around the plate and garnish with mint leaves. Serve with a dish of the remaining pesto alongside.

COMMON WEALTH POULTRY CO.

GARDINER

Ryan Wilson and Gina Simmons started raising ducks in 2010 in response to a growing demand among Maine's high-end restaurants.

In 2011, on land purchased in partnership with Ryan's family, the fledgling farm raised a total of 3,000 birds: 2,000 meat ducks and another thousand birds consisting of chickens, holiday geese, and laying hens. They processed all their animals in an on-site facility.

In ten years, Common Wealth Poultry Co. has grown to a company of 30 employees and processes 300,000 all-natural, additive-free, halal chickens, ducks, turkeys, rabbits, and game fowl per year from their slaughterhouse in Gardiner.

The company not only provides quality, locally raised meats to restaurants, but has developed an easy-to-use e-commerce website that facilitates sales directly to households.

Ryan maintains that his company exists not only to produce high-quality meat products, but to "affect as many people's lives as positively as possible."

Herb-Crusted Leg of Lamb

SERVES 4 TO 6

It doesn't get much simpler than this roasted lamb, but keep an eye on the internal temperature of the meat. Try serving this with Young Carrots with Lemon, Thyme, and Olive Oil (page 80) or, for a special spring meal, Erin French's Spring Bread Salad with Asparagus, Radishes, Peas & Mint (page 67).

8 cloves garlic, peeled and crushed

6 sprigs fresh marjoram

6 dried bay leaves

1 handful fresh thyme sprigs

¼ cup olive oil

1 teaspoon sea salt

Freshly ground black pepper

1 leg of lamb, about 6 pounds, bone-in, trimmed and tied (if you are buying your meat at a local market, you can ask the butcher to do this)

2 tablespoons balsamic vinegar

1. Preheat the oven to 450°F.

2. Place all of the garlic and 4 sprigs of marjoram in a heavy roasting pan. Add 3 bay leaves and about ⅓ of the thyme sprigs. Drizzle 2 tablespoons of the olive oil over the herbs.

3. Strip the leaves from the remaining thyme sprigs, reserving 2 sprigs for garnish. In a small bowl, mix the thyme leaves, the remaining olive oil, sea salt, and a few turns of freshly ground pepper. Rub this mixture all over the meat, making sure to scrape all the herbs and spices out of the bowl. Place lamb on top of herbs in the roasting pan.

4. Roast the lamb for 20 minutes, then turn the oven down to 350°F, pour the balsamic vinegar over the lamb, and roast for about 1 to 1½ hours longer. Turn the leg occasionally and baste with the liquid in the roasting pan.

5. If you are shooting for medium-rare, take the meat out when the internal temperature reads 125°F (the temperature will increase to 130°F as it rests).

6. Let the meat rest for 10 minutes before slicing. Place the slices on a serving dish and garnish with the remaining herbs.

ROARING LION FARM

SEDGWICK

You have to get up pretty early to beat a Mainer to breakfast, but the egg sandwich at Roaring Lion Farm & Market, made with farmer Colin Smorawski's fresh, hand-mixed pork sausage, is worth missing out on a little morning sleep.

"Meishan pork has the right amount of fat," Arianna Smorawski explains. "And Colin's seasoning blend makes it the perfect breakfast patty."

The couple, who met in 2013 when Colin was just getting the farm started, raises heritage Meishan pigs, as well as grass-fed beef, pasture-raised poultry and eggs, and organic market vegetables on their 95-acre farm along the Bagaduce River.

"The Meishan pigs and our cows are the stars of the farm," Arianna says. The couple began by raising just four pigs each year—enough for their own household and a bit left over to sell with their CSA farm shares. The farm now raises 60 pigs per year from their own breeding stock and are currently the only breeders of registered Meishans in the Northeast.

Arianna and Colin sell their meat, eggs, and produce to local restaurants and to their local community at the farm's on-site market and eatery. According to Arianna, the farm, market, and eatery are the result of the couple's commitment to lead a self-reliant and sustainable life that they could share with their community.

It was a dream that they almost walked away from when their son Otto was born with a rare terminal brain condition in 2016.

"We came home from the hospital with him on hospice with a life expectancy of a couple weeks," Arianna recounts. "We thought about quitting farming . . . but realized [he] made our drive and determination stronger."

The Smorawskis add to their pastures and

growing spaces every year, building on their market vegetable offerings and livestock.

Although, Arianna admits, "We could both just watch the cows all day; the way they interact, their excited running dance when on new pasture, and, best of all, the calves playing with each other during early summer 'magic hours.'"

Pork Chops in Creamy Pepper Sauce

SERVES 4

A Maine pig farmer once told me that pork "has twice the flavor of beef at half the price." Even if we don't all have access to heritage varieties such as the Meishan pigs at Roaring Lion Farm, fresh, locally farmed pork—raised in pastures and Maine forests—is healthful and versatile for year-round dining.

Serve these chops tableside, directly from the skillet. You'll be glad to have the creamy sauce—spiked with briny green peppercorns—just an arm's length away so that you can easily ladle more of it over the meat and pretty much anything else on your plate.

4 thick-cut pork chops, about 7 ounces each

Sea salt, to taste

Freshly ground black pepper, to taste

2 tablespoons olive oil

1 large shallot

½ cup dry white wine

1 cup beef stock

7 tablespoons heavy cream

1 tablespoon green peppercorns in brine, rinsed and drained

1 young leek, sliced lengthwise into very thin strips about 1½ inches long

1. Preheat the oven to 275°F.

2. Season the pork with sea salt and freshly ground black pepper. Heat the olive oil over medium-high heat in a cast-iron skillet large enough to fit all of the chops without crowding. Sear the chops in the skillet for 2 to 3 minutes on each side, or until nicely browned. Remove the chops from the pan and place in a roasting pan fitted with a rack. Cook the chops for about 20 minutes, or until the internal temperature reaches 145°F.

3. While the chops are roasting, peel the shallot and chop finely. Return the cast-iron skillet to the stove over medium heat and sauté the shallot in the meat juices until very soft. Pour in the white wine and beef stock. Bring to a boil and reduce until slightly thickened—about 10 minutes.

4. Remove the pan from the heat and push the sauce through a sieve. Return the sauce to the pan, add the cream, and heat to a simmer. Add the green peppercorns and season with salt.

5. Arrange with the pork chops over the sauce directly in the skillet, garnish with strips of leek, and serve.

Autumn Harvest Roast Pork

SERVES 6

Make one weekend trip to a Maine farmers' market in the fall and you'll find all the meat and produce you need for for this dead simple, sheet-pan meal. Grab a fresh loaf of crusty bread from your favorite bakery and maybe add a simple warm side of buttered farro for company.

Rolled pork shoulder, about 3 pounds, trimmed and butterflied

8 cloves garlic, peeled

Sea salt, to taste

Freshly ground black pepper, to taste

2 tablespoon sunflower oil

2 teaspoons chopped fresh thyme leaves

4 large pears, peeled, cored, and quartered

2 large parsnips, peeled and cut into long strips

2 large white potatoes, peeled and cut into wedges

3 tablespoons olive oil

2 tablespoons balsamic vinegar

1. Preheat the oven to 400°F. Line a sheet pan with parchment paper.

2. Open up the pork shoulder on a chopping board. Crush four of the garlic cloves and smear over the pork meat. Season the meat generously with sea salt and freshly ground black pepper, and then re-roll and tie the roast securely at intervals using kitchen twine. Rub the outside of the pork with the sunflower oil, thyme, and plenty more salt and pepper.

3. In a large bowl, toss the remaining garlic cloves with the pears, parsnips, potatoes, olive oil, balsamic vinegar, salt, and pepper. Spill the vegetables in an even layer on the sheet pan.

4. Sit the pork on top of the vegetables and roast for 30 minutes. Reduce the oven heat to 350°F, and cook for 1 hour, or until the internal temperature of the pork reads 145°F.

5. Remove the pan from the oven and cover loosely with aluminum foil. Allow to rest for 15 minutes before serving.

PRIMO RESTAURANT

ROCKLAND

Founded in 2000 as an Italian-inspired local eatery with an on-site vegetable garden, Primo has since become the benchmark of high-end farm-to-table cooking in Maine. Two-time James Beard Award-winning chef Melissa Kelly, who started the restaurant with a cooking staff of three, now leads a team of 60, and the restaurant grounds include two greenhouses, three acres of rotating vegetable crops, 200 laying hens, 150 broiler chickens, 15 pigs, and several ducks.

The restaurant itself has grown and evolved much like the gardens; diversified and sustainable, featuring separate dining rooms within the large Victorian house that cater to the varying tastes of their guests and the spirit of the occasion.

The menu is subject to what is coming out of the garden on any given day, and what the restaurant can source from other local farms and gardens. The distinctly Mediterranean dishes are punctuated by house-made pastas, fresh, local seafood, house-cured charcuterie, and wood-fired pizzas; and many are studded with wild foraged ingredients such as mushrooms, ramps, and nettles.

In the two decades since Primo's inception, Melissa has opened two other Primo Restaurants in partnership with Marriott—Primo Orlando and Primo Tucson. Both are committed to the same farm-to-table philosophy as the original.

Individual Pork Pies with Cranberries

MAKES 12 SMALL PIES

Leaf lard, the high-quality fat rendered from the soft meat surrounding the kidneys and the loin of the pig, is coveted by pastry chefs for flaky, tender crusts. Once considered unhealthy, leaf lard is having its moment with keto devotees and those in search of non-hydrogenated cooking fats. Look for leaf lard at your local farmers' markets, gourmet markets, or at the corner bodega. Serve these festive pies at an informal Christmas Day gathering, to neighbors or carolers stopping by, or as part of the main mid-day meal. They can be made ahead of time, and reheated just to take the chill off. The pickled onion and mustard are a must!

Pork Filling

1¼ pounds lean ground pork

7 ounces fatty bacon, minced

2 large shallots, finely chopped

1 tablespoon Worcestershire sauce

½ teaspoon sea salt

½ teaspoon freshly ground black pepper

1 teaspoon ground allspice

Pastry

6¾ cups all-purpose flour

1 teaspoon sea salt

1 cup water

1 cup leaf lard

1 egg, beaten

Cranberry Topping

2 cups fresh cranberries

⅓ cup sugar

4 tablespoons redcurrant jelly

1 tablespoon lemon juice

1. Preheat the oven to 350°F. Grease a 12-cavity muffin tin and place it on a sheet pan.

2. To make the filling: In a large bowl, mix together the ground pork, minced bacon, shallots, Worcestershire sauce, sea salt, black pepper, and allspice. Set aside.

3. To make the pastry: Sift the flour and salt into a warmed mixing bowl and make a well in the center.

4. Place the water and lard in a pan and bring to a boil. Pour the hot mixture immediately into the well, stirring vigorously to form a dough.

5. Turn the dough out onto a floured board and, as soon as it is comfortable to handle, knead until pliable and soft. Do not allow the pastry to cool too much and do not use while still very hot, or the dough will collapse during shaping. It should be pleasantly warm. Wrap ⅓ of the dough in plastic wrap and set aside in a warm place.

6. Roll out the remaining ⅔ of dough about a ⅛-inch thickness on a lightly floured surface. Cut out 4½-inch rounds using a pastry cutter. Line each cavity of the muffin tin with the rounds, pressing them in and leaving a slight overhang.

7. Divide the filling between the pastry cups, pressing down lightly.

8. Roll out the remaining dough on a floured surface and stamp out 3-inch rounds. Brush the overhanging edges of the filled cases with beaten egg, then put lids on top. Pinch together and crimp the edges with your fingers. Brush the tops with some of the beaten egg.

9. Bake for 30 minutes, then remove the pan from the oven. Remove the pies from the tin and place

them on the sheet pan. Brush the sides and tops again with the rest of the beaten egg, and place the pan back in the oven.

10. Increase the oven temperature to 400°F and bake for another 25 to 30 minutes, or until the glaze is set and pies are deep golden brown all over. Cool them on the sheet pan for a few minutes, then transfer them to a wire rack and cool completely.

11. To make the topping: Place the cranberries and sugar in a medium saucepan and just cover with cold water.

12. Heat until the sugar dissolves and the cranberries pop. Remove the pan from the heat and drain the cranberries in a metal sieve and cool.

13. When the cranberries are cool, arrange them over the top of the pies. Gently heat the redcurrant jelly and lemon juice until melted and bubbling. Stir the mixture until smooth and brush over the cranberries. Serve the pies at room temperature with pickled onions and grainy mustard alongside.

Roast Chicken with Rosemary and Tomatoes

SERVES 4

Refrigerated crates of fresh whole and cut-up chickens are ubiquitous at Maine's year-round farmers' markets, stacked in stalls alongside cartons of eggs and chalkboards listing the availability of specific cuts. Bone-in thighs and drumsticks are great choices for chicken dishes that require few ingredients. The slightly darker meat and thicker bones guarantee lots of flavor and a tender bite. Cooking up both saucy and golden, this simple chicken dish can be assembled in minutes and taken out of the oven in less than an hour, making it a reliable weekday dinner.

2 chicken thighs, trimmed of excess fat

2 chicken drumsticks, trimmed of excess fat

1 pint cherry tomatoes

4 sprigs fresh rosemary

⅔ cup low-sodium chicken stock

2 tablespoons olive oil

Sea salt and freshly ground black pepper, to taste

1. Preheat the oven to 350°F.

2. Sit the chicken pieces, skin side facing down, in a roasting pan and arrange the cherry tomatoes around them. Strip the leaves from two sprigs of rosemary and scatter them over the meat and vegetables.

3. Pour in the stock and then drizzle everything with the olive oil. Season with the sea salt and freshly ground black pepper.

4. Roast, uncovered, for 50 to 55 minutes, or until the chicken is golden on top and cooked through, turning halfway through so that the skin side faces up. Remove the dish from the oven and leave it to stand for 5 minutes.

5. Serve garnished with the remaining rosemary sprigs.

ORCHARD RIDGE FARM

GORHAM

If there's a magic formula for making a successful go at small-scale farming, Steven and Amy Bibula have found it in this simple edict: "Give the people what they want."

When the Bibulas bought 40 acres of Gorham farmland in 2011, they began their venture as a members-only vegetable CSA. By 2013, they were offering their produce, as well as meats and other goods from nearby farms, to the general public at a newly built store on the farm.

Always listening to their customers, who came from all over southern Maine to shop, the Bibulas started converting much of their land over to high bush blueberries, raspberries, and apple trees for the summer and fall "pick-your-own" business. The PYO crowd in turn wanted to buy ready-made treats after a day in the orchards and berry fields, so the couple put in a commercial kitchen and now serves an eclectic menu of take-out, pastries, and breads made with ingredients from theirs and other local farms.

And as backyard chickens gained popularity in recent years, Steven started raising a variety of breeds for live sales. The farm now offers live ducks, geese, chickens, and heritage turkeys—as well as lots of advice on how to raise them.

These days, you can find the farm and market bustling throughout the year, providing farm-fresh groceries and prepared foods to a loyal community of customers.

Pan-Roasted Duck Breast with Chestnuts and Brussels Sprouts

SERVES 4

Duck cuts of all kinds are readily available year-round at Maine's farmers' markets. This recipe is best in the fall, when fresh chestnuts are available in the markets and just-picked Brussels sprouts are sold both loose and on the stalk. Of course, if you can't find fresh chestnuts, canned chestnuts will do just fine, with the added bonus of not having to shell them.

2 cups Brussels sprouts, trimmed and
    scored on their undersides

2 cups fresh chestnuts, shells scored with an X

4 boneless duck breasts, about 7 ounces each

½ teaspoon sea salt

¼ teaspoon freshly ground black pepper

⅓ cup port wine

1⅓ cups chicken stock

Fresh chervil sprigs

1. Slice half of the Brussels sprouts in half and place all of them in a bowl of cold water.

2. Boil the chestnuts in a large saucepan of water for 30 to 40 minutes, or until tender. Drain them and run under water, then remove their shells and set aside.

3. Preheat the oven to 375°F.

4. Over a medium flame, heat a cast-iron pan, large enough to fit the 4 duck breasts, until it's searing hot.

5. Score the fat of the duck breasts in a criss-cross pattern using a sharp knife, and season with the sea salt and pepper. Place them skin-side down into the hot pan, allowing the fat to render.

6. Once the skin has rendered most of its fat and is golden, drain the fat, flip the breasts, and slide the skillet into the oven to finish the cooking; the meat should be firm yet slightly springy to the touch for medium-rare (an internal temperature of 135°F).

7. Remove the duck breasts from the oven, transfer them to a warm plate, and cover loosely with aluminum foil. Allow them to rest for 10 minutes.

8. Meanwhile, drain the Brussels sprouts and bring a large saucepan of salted water to a boil. Add the sprouts to the boiling water and cook for 10 to 12 minutes, or until fork tender, then drain and set aside.

9. While the sprouts are cooking, place the cast-iron skillet over a low heat and deglaze it with the port. Once the wine is reduced by half, add the chicken stock and reduce the liquid by one-third. Add the chestnuts to the sauce to warm through.

10. Slice the duck breasts and arrange on a warmed serving platter. Spoon the Brussels sprouts next to the duck before spooning the sauce and chestnuts over it all.

11. Garnish with sprigs of chervil before serving.

FROM THE PASTURE 145

FROM THE SEA

Lobster accounts for roughly 73 percent of Maine's $700 million commercial fishing industry, with reported landings topping out at just over 100 million pounds in 2019. That's 47 percent of Maine's total commercial fish landings altogether, with bait and oil species taking a distant second, and bivalve species such as mussels, clams, and scallops playing an important if less profitable role as well.

Currently, Maine grows the majority of oysters supplied to the northeast, bringing in over 2 million pounds annually. Growth of the industry has increased fivefold since 2011, and oyster shops have sprouted up in nearly every neighborhood in Maine's largest—and relatively well-heeled—city of Portland.

Seaweed farms, increasingly prevalent in the state's tidal waters, are also well represented on the industry's menu, with harvests accounting for 7 percent of total fishery landings in 2019.

But lobster is the state's crown jewel in what is inarguably a glittering, multi-faceted tiara, earning its place as the top lobster fishery on the planet. And since it's also the most strictly regulated—with well-enforced limits on trap sets and lobster size—that's saying something.

Even among fishermen, a shoreside seafood feast featuring lobsters, clams, mussels, and corn is coastal Maine's go-to welcome meal for visitors. From purchase of the fresh seafood—either from a lobster pound or directly from a harvester—to cooking technique, to eating etiquette, to clean-up, there are few American culinary traditions more celebratory of an area's natural resources than a New England clambake.

ARAGOSTA AT GOOSE COVE LODGE

DEER ISLE

There is a communal table in the center of Devin Finigan's restaurant, Aragosta, that is carved from a single piece of ash and is almost as long as a lobster boat. It is situated on the mezzanine level of the light-filled restaurant and commands a clear view of the wide glittering blue of Penobscot Bay.

Devin sits at the table as if she were in a captain's chair, bright with excitement for the new incarnation of her seven-year-old farm-to-table restaurant.

"This is where the staff will eat," she explains, gesturing to the restaurant's centerpiece. "After prep, before service. My daughters and husband will be here, too. A true family meal."

At first, the polished wood, sparkling chandeliers, and grand staging of the Aragosta's new environs at the lushly refurbished Goose Cove Lodge in Deer Isle seem at odds with Devin's family-centric, direct-from-the-farm philosophy. But as Devin explains, her career in cooking was inspired by her love of entertaining and welcoming people into a beautiful space.

Aragosta's menu is centered around the crustacean for which it's named in Italian—lobsters hauled ashore by her fisherman husband, Luke Hartman. But Devin's Maine-centric inspiration doesn't stop there. The menu reads like a tour through the island and surrounding areas' small family farms: micro greens from Morgan Bay Farms, lamb from David's Folly Farm, beef from a heritage Blonde d'Aquitaine herd in Blue Hill, duck from Bagaduce Farm, and produce from a host of growers including Four Season Farm, Misty Brook Farm, and Fine Line Farm. Devin churns the restaurant's butter from local cream and has plans for harvesting salt from the shore just yards from Aragosta's outside deck.

Aragosta's guests are welcomed with a warm fire in the shoulder-high hearth, freshly baked bread from house-milled wheat, and a five-part amuse bouche that features a taste of whatever is in from the farms and sea that week.

"This is the dream," Devin says of the restaurant and the lodge. "It's the home away from home where my family and I are expecting you."

Aragosta's Blue Hill Bay Mussels with Crispy Kale

SERVES 4 TO 6

Ever since chef Devin Finigan dished out Aragosta's first meals in a tiny dining room looking out over Stonington Harbor, this dish of hyper local rope-grown mussels and garden-fresh aromatics has graced the menu. The addition of deep-fried crispy kale is a creative and fresh stand-in for a Belgian-style moules-&-frites pub dish.

Mussels

3 tablespoons butter

2 cloves garlic, peeled and minced

¼ cup red bell pepper, cut in a ¼-inch dice

¼ cup green bell pepper, cut in a ¼-inch dice

½ leek (white part only), chopped

¼ cup celery, cut in a ¼-inch dice

2 pounds mussels, scrubbed and rinsed, discarding any that don't close when tapped

½ cup dry white wine

4 tablespoons heavy cream

2 tablespoons chopped fresh parley

Crispy Kale

Canola oil, for frying

1 bunch fresh whole kale leaves, washed and dried thoroughly

Kosher salt

1. To make the mussels: Melt the butter over medium-high heat in large, shallow skillet.

2. Add garlic, peppers, leek, and celery. Cook for 2 to 3 minutes until fragrant.

3. Add the mussels, stirring to coat with the pepper mixture. Pour in the white wine and bring it all to a simmer.

4. Cover the pan and steam for 5 to 7 minutes, or until all the mussels open. Throw away any mussels that don't open.

5. Add the heavy cream and parsley to the pan and reduce for 2 to 3 minutes.

6. Scrape everything into a very large serving bowl.

7. To make the kale: While you're reducing the cream for the mussels, begin to heat 2 inches of canola oil in a Dutch oven or cast-iron pot to 375°F.

8. Place the kale leaves in the oil and fry for 1 minute. Work in batches, if necessary, to prevent crowding.

9. Use tongs to transfer them onto paper towels.

10. After sprinkling the leaves with a little Kosher salt, heap them atop the mussels, and serve.

BANGS ISLAND MUSSELS

PORTLAND

Matt Moretti claims the best way to cook a mussel is in the microwave.

"It's the most pure form of eating mussels," claims the good-humored 37-year-old CEO of Bangs Island Mussels. "Especially when they're super fresh. You bring 'em in, toss a handful in the microwave for a minute, they steam in their own juices and open up. It's fast food from the ocean."

With a graduate degree in marine biology and more than 10 years at the helm of the growing multi-trophic aquaculture company, it's actually hard not to trust Matt's unorthodox cooking advice. The guy knows his mussels.

Bangs Island grows their mussels on 35-foot ropes that hang from large rafts made up of a grid of wooden beams and float in the Casco Bay.

"Mussels are the lowest impact food you can find," says Matt, explaining that, grown in this manner, the wild shellfish create reefs—little underwater ecosystems that provide habitat for other marine wildlife.

"The act of growing a mussel is helping improve the environment," he explains.

Each rope on the 40-by-40-foot rafts produces roughly 200 pounds of market-size mussels, and in 2018, the company brought 266,000 pounds of mussels to market.

But Matt says that because mussels are the most inexpensive seafood out there, in order for the company to succeed, they need to keep scaling. In 2020, Bangs Island purchased a neighboring mussel farm, and predicts they will close to quadruple their annual harvest by 2021.

Bangs Island sells 100 percent of its mussel harvests to distributors and wholesalers, who then parcel them out to restaurants in Maine and across the country. The mussels, which are iden-tified by the Bang's Island name on local menus, are distinctive for their larger size—just under three inches—and their high meat to shell ratio.

Matt, who bought Bangs Island Mussels with his dad in 2010, says that they continue to experiment with other types of aquaculture. The company is currently the largest seaweed farm on the east coast of the United States, and is also farming clams and scallops, though—for the moment—on a much smaller scale.

Matt explains that this type of multi-species aquaculture has a doubly positive impact on the environment, because, he says, "You're farming an ecosystem, not just a monoculture."

Mussels and Tomatoes in Beer Sauce

SERVES 4

Fresh, live mussels will add their natural brine to any liquid they're cooked in, so for this dish, choose a beer that is crisp and light, and not too hoppy. There are a multitude of craft varieties in Maine to pick from. If you imbibe, make it one that you'd also like to sip, as hot, steamy mussels and a cold brew are a match made in shoreside heaven. For a light dinner, serve these mussels alongside Potato Wedges with Rosemary (page 86) and make sure to have plenty of bread to mop up the sauce and vegetables.

2½ cups beer

4 to 6 cloves garlic, peeled and minced

1 medium white onion, sliced

1 pint cherry tomatoes, halved

2 tablespoons unsalted butter

Pinch of kosher salt

2 pounds mussels, scrubbed and rinsed, discarding any that don't close when tapped

2 to 3 tablespoons finely chopped fresh parsley

Fresh, crusty bread, for serving

1. In a wide, deep skillet over medium heat, bring the beer, garlic, onion, cherry tomatoes, butter, and a generous pinch of salt to a rapid simmer.

2. Add the mussels, cover the pan, and steam until shells open up, 5 to 7 minutes, until all the mussels have opened.

3. Remove the pan from heat and discard any mussels that haven't opened. Sprinkle the dish with chopped parsley.

4. Divide the mussels and sauce between bowls and serve immediately with plenty of bread on the side.

NONESUCH OYSTER FARM

SCARBOROUGH

The very last person who thought Abigail Carroll would become an oyster farmer was Abigail Carroll.

But when a friend asked to tap into her background in international finance and help him write a business plan for a free-range oyster farm in Maine—and then backed out—Abigail decided to take it on herself.

"I never even had an oyster before I started an oyster farm," Abigail says. "But now I crave them."

Nonesuch Oyster Farm, located in Scarborough Marsh, Maine's largest estuary, produces three varieties of award-winning boutique oysters, which are on the menus of some of the best restaurants in the country.

"The marsh is both salt and fresh water," Abigail explains. "And oysters love that."

When Abigail began the farm in 2010, there weren't a whole lot of people doing it in Maine and she had trouble finding workers.

"It just wasn't a thing in southern Maine," she says.

The upside to that, of course, was that her farm was one of just a few filling a niche, and three years in she was starting to turn a profit.

"Then the Polar Vortex hit in 2014, and it wiped out the entire farm," Abigail recounts.

Rather than call it quits, Abigail said she took her father's advice and "cowboyed up," investing everything she had to buy new gear and seed stock. But by the time the farm was up and running again, the oyster landscape in Maine had shifted.

"The price of oysters has gone down significantly," Abigail explains, citing the spike in new oyster farms up and down the coast. And the competition for market space has increased.

So Abigail decided to innovate, and in 2015 she began offering boat-guided tours of the farm. Small groups of guests learn about, harvest, and eat fresh oysters right out of the marsh. The tours are so popular that the farm raises a single variety of oyster exclusively for tour guests.

Today, Abigail credits the hands-on experiential tours for saving her farm, and allowing her to further innovate her product line. Along with harvesting close to 600,000 oysters annually, she also produces a line of natural algae-based skincare products.

Oysters on the Half Shell with Shallot Mignonette

SERVES 2 TO 4

Visitors to Nonesuch Oyster Farm have the option of reserving space on a boat-guided tour of the oyster flats in Scarborough Marsh where one of the farm's team members will talk about estuarial oyster farming in Maine from nursery to harvest, and help guests harvest and shuck an assortment of fresh-from-the-water oysters to enjoy right there on the boat. This simple mignonette is served "deck-side," and guests are invited to bring aboard their favorite beverage accompaniment.

1 large shallot

¼ cup Prosecco vinegar, or red wine vinegar

Freshly ground black pepper

12 chilled, live oysters, rinsed and scrubbed

Crushed ice

1. Mince the shallot and place it into a ramekin. Pour in the vinegar so that it completely covers the shallot (you may use more or less than ¼ cup). Grind in a couple of turns of black pepper.

2. Shuck the oysters, taking care to not lose any of the brine, and making sure to sever the meat completely free of the shell. Discard the top shell.

3. Place the bottom shell with the meat onto a platter heaped with crushed ice.

4. Serve the oysters family style, allowing your guests to spoon the mignonette onto their own oysters.

Oysters au Gratin

SERVES 4

If you prefer your oysters cooked, this classic appetizer produces an appealing "gratinized" top, without overcooking the oyster beneath. Purchase a larger variety for this dish; in Maine these could be Bagaduce or Pemaquid oysters, 3 to 5 inches in length.

8 live oysters, rinsed and scrubbed

2¼ cups sea salt

1 tablespoon olive oil

1 small shallot, chopped

1 stalk celery, finely diced

½ red pepper, finely diced

1 small carrot, finely diced

⅓ cup dry white wine

Salt

Freshly ground black pepper

⅓ cup whipping cream

1 egg yolk

¼ cup finely grated Parmesan

1. Shuck the oysters, taking care to not lose any of the brine, and making sure to sever the meat completely free of the shell. Rinse the bottom shells and set them aside. Reserve the brine.

2. Fill a casserole dish with the sea salt as a bed. Place the bottom shells in the dish with the open side upwards, so they cannot tip over. Return the oysters to the shells, cover, and chill.

3. Heat the olive oil in a pan and sauté the shallot, celery, red pepper, and carrot over a low heat for 2 to 4 minutes. Deglaze with the white wine and season with salt and ground black pepper. Bring it all to a boil and simmer briefly, then drain the vegetables in a strainer, reserving the liquid.

4. Combine the brine from the oysters and the vegetable cooking liquid with the whipping cream and egg yolk, whisk thoroughly, and season to taste with salt and ground black pepper.

5. Preheat the broiler.

6. Divide the vegetables between the oysters. Top each with the yolk and cream mixture and sprinkle with Parmesan.

7. Place oysters under the broiler for 3 to 5 minutes, or until golden brown. Keep a close watch on the oysters to prevent burning. Serve immediately.

Oysters with Cucumber Sauce

SERVES 4

Shallot-y mignonettes and horseradish-spiked cock-tail sauces aren't everyone's thing. This mild cucumber sauce, seasoned gently with lemon and basil, allows the flavor of the raw oyster and its ocean-y brine to shine through. The coppery bite of Belon oysters are a great choice for this dish, but any small-size oyster will do.

4 Persian cucumbers, finely diced

1 teaspoon fresh lemon juice

¼ teaspoon kosher salt

¼ teaspoon freshly ground black pepper

2 tablespoons fresh basil leaves

3 tablespoons extra virgin olive oil

2 slices white bread, diced into small cubes

12 large live oysters, rinsed and scrubbed

Crushed ice

2 teaspoons fresh oregano leaves

1. Preheat the oven to 375°F.

2. Place three-quarters of the cucumber, the lemon juice, salt, pepper, half the basil leaves, and 2 tablespoons of the olive oil in a food processor. Process until smooth.

3. Pass the sauce through a fine sieve into a small bowl. Cover and chill until needed.

4. In a medium bowl, toss the bread cubes with the remaining oil, and then spill them onto a rimmed baking sheet.

5. Bake the bread cubes in the oven until golden and crisp, 6 to 9 minutes. Remove the pan from the oven and let the croutons cool completely.

6. Shuck the oysters, taking care to not lose any of the brine, and making sure to sever the meat completely free of the shell.

7. Discard the top shells, leaving the oyster and its juices in the bottom half. Arrange them on a platter of crushed ice.

8. Spoon the cucumber sauce into the oyster shells. Garnish with the croutons, remaining diced cucumber, remaining basil leaves, and some oregano leaves. Serve immediately.

HARBOR FISH MARKET

PORTLAND

Ask any resident of Portland where they buy their fresh fish and seafood and most will tell you Harbor Fish.

The Alfiero family has been providing Maine chefs and home cooks with both popular and rare fish for their tables and restaurants from their market and processing center on Custom House Wharf since 1966.

Live lobsters arrive directly from boats to the processing center through the market's back door and are kept in on-site tanks that recirculate seawater directly from the Casco Bay. The market sells lobsters, as it does most of its shellfish, live, cooked, or shucked—whatever their customers might need or want. The market is also known for its popular in-store weekend specials that they post weekly on their Facebook page, along with recipes from the Alfieros' Italian American home kitchens, Harbor Fish employees, and the market's community of customers.

Harbor Fish Market also has a healthy wholesale market, supplying grocery stores and other clientele nationwide.

Fried Clams

SERVES 4

Use soft-shell clams—what are called "steamers"—for fried clams. Their relatively small meats are tender and cook quickly. Dredging fresh, shucked clams in a dry flour-cornmeal mix rather than coating them in batter is the secret to producing an extra crispy fried clam with big clam flavor. Masa harina is extra fine corn flour processed with lime (the mineral, not the fruit), making it more digestible. It is available in most grocery stores these days, but if you can't find it, fine cornmeal will do.

1 cup masa harina (fine, nixtamalized corn flour), or fine cornmeal

1 cup all-purpose flour

1 teaspoon kosher salt

½ teaspoon freshly ground black pepper

¼ teaspoon cayenne pepper

¼ teaspoon paprika

1 cup buttermilk

6 cups canola or vegetable oil, for deep-frying

1½ pounds shucked steamer clams

1 lemon, cut into wedges

1. Stir together the masa harina, flour, salt, pepper, cayenne, and paprika in a shallow dish. Pour the buttermilk into a medium-sized bowl. Line a baking sheet with several layers of paper towels.

2. Preheat the oven to 250°F. Heat the oil in a deep heavy-based saucepan or Dutch oven to 375°F.

3. Add the clams to the buttermilk, gently stirring to coat. With a slotted spoon, scoop them out and into the flour mix. Toss them to coat them thoroughly.

4. When the oil is ready, remove about half the clams from the flour mix and shake off the excess before carefully transferring to the hot oil.

5. Deep-fry until golden and crisp, about 2 minutes, stirring the clams after about 1 minute to separate them and prevent clumping. Transfer the fried clams to the paper towel–lined baking sheet and keep them warm in the oven.

6. Repeat for the remaining clams. Serve immediately with lemon wedges alongside.

Baked Stuffed Clams

SERVES 6 AS AN APPETIZER

Crispy on the outside, steamy on the inside, this hearty appetizer could also serve as a light dinner paired with a big summer salad. Large, hard-shell Quahogs or Hen clams are the best choice for this dish.

12 large, live hard-shell clams (about 3 inches wide)

4 tablespoons butter

½ yellow onion, finely chopped

2 celery stalks, finely diced

Pinch of kosher salt

½ serrano chile, seeds removed and chopped finely

½ red bell pepper, cored, seeded, and finely diced

¼ cup grated Parmesan

½ teaspoon kosher salt

¼ teaspoon freshly ground black pepper

1½ cups bread crumbs

Hot sauce, to taste

1 lemon, cut into wedges

¼ cup fresh dill sprigs

1. In a wide, deep skillet, bring 1¼ cups of water to boil. Add the clams and cover the skillet and steam the clams until they open, 6 to 8 minutes. Discard any clams that did not open.

2. Remove the clams from the skillet and reserve the cooking liquid. Remove the meat from the shells, chop finely, and set aside. Save half of each shell.

3. Preheat the oven to 350°F. Melt 3 tablespoons of the butter in a small saucepan set over a medium flame or in a heatproof bowl in the microwave. Set aside.

4. Melt the remaining butter in a skillet set over a medium flame. Add the onion, celery, and a pinch of salt, cover, and sweat the vegetables until softened, 5 to 6 minutes.

5. Transfer the vegetables to a bowl and let cool for 5 minutes. Stir in the chile pepper, bell pepper, chopped clams, Parmesan, salt, pepper, half the bread crumbs, and some hot sauce to taste. Stir in enough clam cooking liquid to moisten the mixture.

6. Spoon the mixture into the clam shells, and arrange them on a rimmed baking sheet. Top with the remaining bread crumbs and drizzle with the melted butter.

7. Bake until golden brown on top, 20 to 25 minutes. Remove them from the oven and let cool briefly before serving with lemon wedges and a garnish of dill.

Classic Crab Cakes

SERVES 4

If you're looking for a light, fluffy crab cake with lots of other things mixed in, this is not the recipe for you. Instead, these crab cakes deliver fresh crab flavor unencumbered by any number of aromatics and vegetables found in some recipes. Purists will eat these with just a squeeze of lemon and feel like they've won the crab cake lottery.

Most picked crabmeat in Maine comes from rock crabs—nicknamed "peeky-toe" by Portland seafood merchant and entrepreneur Rod Mitchell. The meat is sweet and mild and so coveted it can be hard to find during the summer tourist season when clam shacks are doing brisk business in crab rolls.

16 ounces super fresh crabmeat

1 large egg

¼ cup mayonnaise

1 teaspoon Dijon mustard

1 pinch red pepper flakes

¼ teaspoon paprika

1 pinch celery salt

1 teaspoon lemon juice

½ teaspoon Worcestershire sauce

¼ teaspoon sea salt

1¼ cups fresh bread crumbs

1 tablespoon chopped flat-leaf parsley

2 tablespoons unsalted butter

1 tablespoon olive oil

Lemon wedges

Tartar Sauce (page 183)

1. Place the crabmeat in a large mixing bowl and set aside.

2. In a separate bowl, whisk together the egg, mayonnaise, mustard, red pepper flakes, paprika, celery salt, lemon juice, Worcestershire sauce, and sea salt. Scrape this mixture into the bowl with the crabmeat and stir until well combined.

3. Add the bread crumbs and parsley to the bowl and mix well. Cover with plastic wrap and chill for 1 hour.

4. Shape the crab mixture into 8 cakes, approximately 1 inch thick.

5. Heat the butter and oil in a large frying pan and add the crab cakes. Cook for 4 to 5 minutes until golden brown on the base, then turn the cakes over, reduce the heat, and cook until golden brown.

6. Serve with lemon wedges and tartar sauce.

Haddock and Corn Chowder

SERVES 6

There is some debate among Maine fishermen about whether corn belongs in fish chowder. Personally, I can't resist the nubbly texture that kernels give the soup and the pop of color and crunch swimming around in all that thick, satiny milk. Cooks on the coast tend not to thicken their chowders with flour and rely instead on the viscosity of evaporated milk to give the soup body. And so that's how we've done it here, resulting in a melt-in-your-mouth, non-gritty texture that can hold up to several re-heatings. If at all possible, make the chowder the day before you plan to serve it; it really tastes best having had a day to cure in the refrigerator.

4 slices bacon

1 medium yellow onion, chopped

2 ribs celery, finely diced

3 cups bottled clam juice

3 medium potatoes, peeled and cut in a ½-inch dice

2 cups corn kernels, fresh or frozen

3 cups evaporated milk

2 tablespoons unsalted butter

1 teaspoon Worcestershire sauce

Sea salt, to taste

Freshly ground black pepper, to taste

2 pounds fresh haddock

Several pinches paprika

1 tablespoon finely chopped fresh parsley

1. In a soup pot or Dutch oven, cook the bacon slices over medium heat for about 10 minutes, turning once, until crispy. Remove the bacon and drain on paper towels. Chop it, and set it aside.

2. Add the chopped onion and celery to the bacon drippings and cook for about 10 minutes, or until soft and translucent.

3. Add the clam juice and the potatoes to the pot and bring to a boil, reduce the heat to low, and simmer for 8 minutes. Add the corn kernels and continue to cook for 6 minutes, or until the potatoes are tender.

4. When the potatoes are soft, add the evaporated milk, butter, Worcestershire sauce, salt, and pepper to the pot and heat until steaming. Add the chopped bacon and the haddock, and simmer until the fish is cooked through—about 7 minutes.

5. Break up the haddock a bit if it hasn't fallen apart on its own. Check the seasoning of the soup, and adjust if necessary. Season with paprika. If more liquid is needed, add a little water or more evaporated milk.

6. Serve immediately or cool and store covered in the refrigerator overnight. Reheat gently.

Cream of Lobster Soup

SERVES 4

If you ever steam live lobsters, reserve those shells! You can turn them immediately into seafood stock or place them in zippered plastic bags and freeze them to make stock later. It will make all the difference in a soup like this one.

4 tablespoons unsalted butter

1 white onion, finely chopped

1 carrot, peeled and finely chopped

2 celery stalks, finely chopped

Pinch of sea salt, plus more to taste

2 cloves garlic, minced

1 tablespoon tomato paste

4 cups fish or seafood stock (homemade or bottled)

1 cup dry white wine

¼ cup dry sherry

1 bay leaf

3 fresh thyme sprigs

⅔ cup heavy cream

1 pound cooked lobster meat, roughly chopped

Freshly ground black pepper, to taste

¼ cup fresh tarragon sprigs

1 lemon, sliced

1. Melt the butter in a Dutch oven or heavy-bottomed soup pot set over a medium flame.

2. Stir in the onion, carrot, celery, and a pinch of salt, and sweat until softened, 7 to 9 minutes.

3. Stir in the garlic and tomato paste, cooking and stirring occasionally until the paste has darkened a little, about 2 minutes.

4. Stir in the stock, wine, sherry, bay leaf, and thyme sprigs, and bring to a boil over a medium heat.

5. Once boiling, reduce the heat to low and gently simmer for 30 minutes, stirring from time to time.

6. Discard the bay leaf and thyme sprigs before pureeing the soup with an immersion blender; you can also do this step in a food processor or blender working in two batches. Push the puree through a fine-mesh sieve.

7. Return the soup to a very gentle simmer and stir in the cream and lobster meat, warming through for 5 minutes. Season to taste with salt and pepper.

8. Ladle into bowls and garnish with tarragon sprigs and lemon slices.

JASON BARTER, FISHERMAN

ISLE AU HAUT

Travel out to Isle au Haut, one of Maine's 15 unbridged, year-round islands, and you'll likely run into a Barter. Currently spanning four generations, the family has been the backbone of the island's lobstering fleet since the 1700s—and if fisherman Jason Barter is any indication, they don't show signs of stopping.

Grandson to Billy Barter, the family's 83-year-old patriarch, Jason started fishing just about as soon as he could walk onto his grandfather's boat, the FV *Islander*. He got his first fishing license at age six, and, with Billy's help, hand-hauled a few lobster traps from a 12-foot skiff. He graduated to 14-foot outboard at age 12, and then an 18-footer at age 16.

Now, at 41, Jason fishes year-round from a 36-foot Crowley Beal, the FV *Islander II*, and still reserves a few days a week during the summer to haul with Billy.

"I've learned everything I know from my grandfather," Jason says.

A father to two teenagers and a toddler, Jason provides for his family by lobstering year-round from the *Islander II*. He also helps out aboard fellow fisherman Lincoln Tully's FV *High Islander* during the winter scallop season. In the spring, Jason gets a state license for the short halibut season and splits his time between shore-bound lobster trap repair and pursuing the profitable fish coveted by chefs around the state.

Jason, along with most Isle au Haut fishermen, sells his catch in Stonington, and contributes up to 42,000 pounds of lobster to the town's top-rated annual landings.

But if you're lucky enough to spend a night or two on Isle au Haut in the summer and get a hankering for lobster, most folks will give you Jason's number, as he generally has a stash tied up to the town float.

Tall and broad-shouldered, Jason has a quick smile and the carefree air of someone who never had to figure out what he wanted to be when he grew up.

"I love fishing," Jason says, "Love it. I like being my own boss. And you never know what's gonna come up in the traps. And as far as workplace, well, it's the prettiest spot to be."

Steamed Maine Lobster

SERVES 6

There might be lots of debate about how to cook a lobster in other places, but not in Maine. In Maine, we steam our lobsters. It's quick, requires no more than a large pot, and produces sweet, tender meat.

Most fishermen I know are militant about removing the bands as they place the lobsters in the pot. They claim that boiled rubber doesn't do anything for the flavor of the lobster. So, if you are deft enough, I recommend you do this. However, if you are nervous about being pinched, go ahead and leave them on. I personally have never noticed much of a difference in the flavor of banded versus un-banded lobsters.

If you are serving hard-shell lobsters, supply each of your guests with a cracker. No need for a cracker if serving shedders—or soft-shell lobsters. The shells will easily tear, revealing the extra sweet, tender meat that shedders are known for.

If you are entertaining guests who are unfamiliar with eating lobster, it's hospitable to give the group a lesson on how to best enjoy their meal. New to lobster yourself? You can find plenty of tutorials online which will teach you how to eat a lobster like you were born in downeast Maine.

You'll probably want to purchase more lobsters than you and your guests will eat so that you can pick out the meat from the remainders and use it to make Luke's Lobster Rolls (page 172), El El Frijoles Lobster Tacos (page 174), or any number of other recipes that call for fresh lobster meat!

6 live Maine lobsters, 1½ pounds each

8 ounces butter, melted

Fresh lemons, halved

1. Place 2 to 3 inches of water in a large pot. If you have a steamer rack large enough, you could use it here, but you really don't need it. Cover the pot and bring the water to a rolling boil. The pot should build up a full head of steam before you add the lobsters.

2. Carefully, place the live lobsters one at a time into the pot, removing the bands as you go. Cover the pot and cook for 14 to 20 minutes. Halfway through the cooking process, carefully lift the lid (steam is very hot) and shift the lobsters around to promote even cooking.

3. The lobster shells will be bright red and the tails will be curled when they are done. Pull on one of the lobsters' long antennae; it should release easily if they are fully cooked.

4. Using tongs or gloved hands, take the lobsters out of the pot, remove the bands if you haven't already done so, and allow the lobster to rest for about 4 to 5 minutes before serving.

5. Meanwhile, melt the butter and divide it between individual bowls or ramekins. Halve the lemons. Place the lobsters on a platter and serve hot with melted butter and lemons.

LUKE'S LOBSTER
SACO AND PORTLAND

In 2009, Ben Conniff responded to a Craigslist want ad and a month later was opening the first Luke's Lobster—a 200-square-foot Maine-style lobster shack—in New York City.

The Maine-based business, co-founded by Ben and Luke Holden, who did in fact meet each other through Craigslist, specializes in small-format restaurants with a limited menu of seafood rolls, soups, and salads. Since opening that first shack in the East Village, the company has grown to over 40 restaurants in the United States, Japan, Taiwan, Korea, Singapore, and the United Kingdom.

In 2013, Luke's Lobster opened a seafood processing plant in Saco, Maine, where they process over 5 million pounds of live lobsters annually.

"Most of the lobsters caught in Maine are new shell," Ben, the company co-founder and chief marketing officer, explains. "Processing takes [soft-shell] lobster that can't survive travel, or lobster that is in excess of what the live market would be able to sell, and turns it into value-added products. Which generally means frozen raw tails and cooked knuckle and claw meat."

For Luke's, it also means they can ensure the quality of 100 percent of the lobster they ship to their restaurants all over the world. At the plant they are able to humanely separate the body from the tail and then cook each of the lobster's parts for the correct amount of time. This results in lobster meat harvested and cooked at the prime of the lobster's life, says Ben, and not harvested from live lobsters whose tissues have degraded by being held in a tank or on refrigerated trucks during travel.

The company prides itself on the quality, traceability, and sustainability of its seafood, and the direct relationships they have with the fishermen.

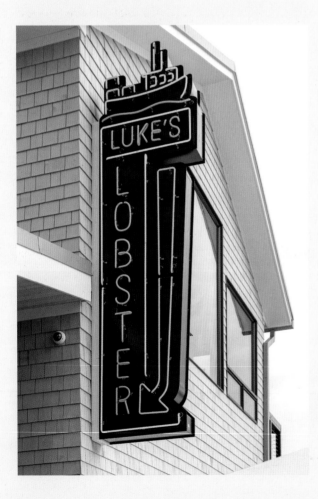

Ben says that for a lot of growth-stage restaurants, these types of values might get diluted with fast expansion; for Luke's, it's been the opposite.

"Growing a certain number of locations allowed us to justify having our own seafood processing company," explains Ben. "Having our own seafood processing company allowed us to have much more direct conversation and relationships with lobstermen. Having direct relationships with lobstermen has reinforced the importance of this industry, in their sustainable practices, and supporting their community."

Luke's buys from town lobster co-ops up and down the coast of Maine, and Ben estimates that their purchases directly impact up to 140 Maine families. The company even helped found the Tenants Harbor Fisherman's Co-op at Miller's Wharf in St. George and buys 100 percent of what they catch. The Co-op helped to bring the family-owned wharf out of hard times, and the opening of a seasonal Luke's Lobster shack at the Co-op has further rejuvenated the town's waterfront.

In their tenth year, Luke's opened their 4,500-square-foot flagship restaurant in the very heart of Portland's working waterfront. The restaurant serves a full menu, has a bar, ample seating, and unbeatable views of Casco Bay and beyond. The restaurant also serves as a landing dock for Portland lobstermen and a venue for wintertime educational events.

"If you had asked me 10 years ago, I would have said I don't have any interest in running a large company," says Ben. "But as we got to see the positive impact that came with the growth of the company, we all got more comfortable continuing to grow. It's scary, but it also feels good to write 600 paychecks each week and to touch that many people's lives."

Luke's Lobster Rolls

SERVES 2

In Luke's Lobster co-founder Ben Conniff's opinion, tail meat has no place in a lobster roll. The popular Maine-based lobster shack company makes its signature roll with only the tender knuckle and claw meat. The recipe calls for Luke's special secret seasoning, which you can purchase directly from the company's website. If you'd rather make your own seasoning mix, stir together a little celery seed powder, sea salt, and just a dash of garlic powder. After you've sprinkled a little on top of your lobster roll, store the remainders in a tightly sealed jar with a plastic lid.

1 tablespoon salted butter

2 New England-style split-top hot dog buns

1 teaspoon mayonnaise

8 ounces fresh, cooked lobster knuckle and claw meat

¼ teaspoon freshly squeezed lemon juice

Luke's Lobster Seasoning Mix (optional)

1. In a small saucepan, melt the butter over low heat. Remove from the heat and brush half a teaspoon of melted butter onto the outer sides of your buns, saving the rest of the butter for later.

2. Heat a small pan over medium-low heat for 1 minute, then toast the buns in the pan until golden brown, 1 to 2 minutes per side. Remove the buns from the pan and place on a plate.

3. Spread ½ teaspoon of the mayonnaise on the inside of each bun.

4. Fill each bun with half of the lobster meat.

5. Reheat the remaining melted butter, if necessary, and add the lemon juice. Drizzle the warm lemon butter evenly over the lobster in each sandwich.

6. Evenly sprinkle one pinch of Luke's Seasoning on top of sandwich (if using). Serve immediately.

EL EL FRIJOLES

SARGENTVILLE

Locating El El Frijoles, one of Maine's most unusual hidden culinary destinations, will depend heavily on what time of year you find yourself on Route 15, deep in the heavily wooded folds of the Blue Hill Peninsula. In the summer, you'll know the place by the crowds of people convivially lined up outside a classic New England–style barn. But in winter, you'll have to keep a lookout for the restaurant's beloved roadside sign—a red lobster in a taco shell painted on a bright yellow background.

From the outside, El El Frijoles looks much like any Maine barn converted to capture seasonal business—the kind that sell antiques in the summer and apples in the fall. But step inside and you'll find a distinctly San Francisco–style taqueria, bustling with a quick-moving crew behind a bright counter, wrapping giant burritos, folding fish-laden tacos, or tossing fresh cabbage salads garnished with guacamole.

"There's this perception that good food can only be found in fine-dining restaurants," says Michael Rossney, who owns the restaurant with his wife, chef Michele Levesque. "Our goal was to provide good-quality food at an affordable price point."

Michael and Michele met in the San Francisco Bay Area and moved to Maine as newlyweds in the early 2000s. Their dream to open a casual California-style taqueria that served ultra-fresh affordable food manifested by 2007 into the barn on their Sargentville property.

Michele, an art educator who learned "fish everything" by working in the seafood markets of her home state of Rhode Island, admits she had no idea how to source ingredients for a Mexican restaurant in rural Maine. So she turned to her neighbors—fishermen, farmers, cheese makers—and built a creative, but distinctly Mexican menu around what they produced.

The hand-lettered chalkboard above the service counter at El El Frijoles lays out a menu of taqueria standbys heavily infused with the Maine-flavored twists the restaurant is famous for, including the house special—a garlic and achiote-spiced lobster taco on Michele's handmade corn tortillas. Even the name of their restaurant has a local twist—a play on the iconic Maine outdoor gear retailer, L.L.Bean.

The restaurant, well into its second decade, has built their success not only on their reputation for excellent food and their support of local agriculture, but also by practicing a deeply authentic philosophy of giving back to their small community. The couple and a small crew of volunteers band together for a few Sundays each summer to host a special dinner event they call "Sunday Suppers for a Cause." The dinners comprise a once-only menu that utilizes some of Michele's more creative skills and veers dramatically from the taqueria menu. One hundred percent of the proceeds are donated to a neighboring community project. For a restaurant that depends heavily on the fierce loyalty of a relatively small population of year-round locals, this kind of goodwill goes a long way.

"Living in a small community can sometimes feel a little insular," Michael says, referring to an attitude of fierce self-reliance prevalent in rural Maine. "We wanted to challenge our neighbors—and ourselves—to think a little bit bigger. We believe that helping out your neighbors can be a unifying force."

El El Frijoles Lobster Tacos

SERVES 3, OR MAKES 9 INDIVIDUAL TACOS

Lobster meat yield from shell-on lobsters varies greatly from season to season. Hard-shell lobsters (generally available year-round) yield more meat than soft-shell lobsters (available only during shedding season in mid- to late-summer). But a general rule of thumb is that for 1 pound of picked lobster meat, you'll need 5 to 6 pounds of soft-shell lobsters, or 4½ to 5½ pounds of hard-shell lobster. Of course, most coastal fish shops also sell fresh, picked lobster meat at a premium price. My own local fish shop, Harbor Fish Market (page 159), sells cooked and chilled shell-on lobsters at a very good price and, as I currently live in a small, not-very-well-ventilated apartment, this is my favorite way to buy them. I use the spent shells to make seafood stock, which I can then use for recipes like Cream of Lobster Soup (page 167), or Haddock and Corn Chowder (page 166).

Ensalada de la Paz

2 cups shredded green cabbage

1 teaspoon kosher salt

Juice from 1 lime

½ jalapeño chile, seeded and finely diced

1 medium tomato, chopped

2 tablespoons finely chopped cilantro

½ small red onion, finely diced

Crema

3 tablespoons milk

1 cup full-fat sour cream

Lobster Filling and Assembly

3 tablespoons Spiced Achiote Butter (page 212)

1 pound freshly cooked and picked lobster meat (see headnote)

9 corn tortillas

1 ripe avocado, pitted, peeled, and sliced

Red Onion and Jalapeño Quick Pickle (page 288)

1. To make the the ensalada, toss the cabbage with the salt and lime juice in a medium bowl and allow it to sit for 10 minutes, or until the cabbage begins to soften.

2. Add the jalapeño, tomato, cilantro, and red onion. Stir together and taste. You may add additional lime or salt to your liking. Set aside.

3. To make the crema, stir the milk into the sour cream until smooth. Set aside.

4. Melt the Spiced Achiote Butter in a large saucepan. Add the lobster and continue to stir until the meat is just warmed through. Don't overcook or the lobster will become rubbery.

5. To assemble the tacos, lay out three tortillas on each plate. Evenly distribute the lobster among the tortillas. Drizzle with any extra butter from the pan. Top each taco with 2 to 3 tablespoons of ensalada, 3 slices of avocado, a tablespoon of Red Onion and Jalapeño Quick Pickle, and a small dollop of crema. Serve immediately.

LINDA GREENLAW WESSEL, FISHERMAN

SURRY

In the two-plus decades since Sebastian Junger's book *The Perfect Storm* placed Maine-raised swordboat captain Linda Greenlaw in the public eye, she has published five best-selling nonfiction books about life as a commercial fisherman, three mystery novels, and two cookbooks.

Through it all, Linda has continued her career on the water—fishing out of ports up and down the East Coast. Now retired from captaining large boats, Linda hauls 350 traps from her 41-foot wooden lobster boat *Earnest* out of her home port in Surry, Maine.

"It amounts to two very long days of hauling each week, but it's perfect. I've got lots of other things to do," says Linda, who works as a broker at her husband Steve Wessel's boat-building business and who also continues to write books on the side.

But it's clear that Linda's first love is fishing. She sells most of her catch to the owner of the neighborhood lobster shack, an enterprising businessman who hustles a wholesale business on the side, and who also partners with Linda for a popular Lobster 101 summer charter business for tourists curious about lobstering.

Linda began her career as a mess cook on a swordboat at the age of 19 and rose through the ranks to eventually become known as one of the

best swordboat captains in the industry. She spent most of her career off-shore for 10 to 30 days at a time fishing for sword or lobster.

"Hundred-foot boats, big crews, 3,000 traps," she recounts.

But these days, Linda enjoys a much slower pace on the water.

"There's no white knuckle hurry-up, yellin' at the sternman," Linda jokes. "I enjoy it."

Linda comes from a long line of passionate cooks who love to entertain. She's written two cookbooks with her mother, Martha, which have been hailed as "must-have" by *Time Magazine*. And she's well-known for her dinner parties, which always feature the freshest fish available.

But Linda claims that the best place to eat a lobster is with friends aboard her boat.

"I bring a gas cooker and we steam our haul right there on deck," Linda explains. "I empty the cooked lobsters out on the washboard and we dig in. No plates, no utensils. I just hose it all down when we're done."

Linda's enthusiasm for fishing is infectious, and she claims it's an industry driven by "eternal optimism."

"As long as you have one more buoy to haul, there's always reason to hope," she says. "Or there's always tomorrow, or there's always next season. Fishing in general is the epitome of optimism."

Lobster Carbonara

SERVES 8

Linda claims this is her favorite lobster dish, and it comes to her from good friend and neighbor Donna Doyen. The list of ingredients is long, and the preparation does take some time and care, but the resulting dish—bursting with texture and the fresh flavors of summer—is fancy dinner party–worthy. Donna admits, however, that if the night is too crazy, she might skip the egg on top.

6 ears corn

8 eggs

1½ pounds fresh, picked lobster meat

Juice of 1 large lemon

4 slices bacon or pancetta

1 white onion, finely chopped

¼ cup chopped garlic

1 teaspoon fresh thyme leaves

2 bay leaves

1 teaspoon freshly ground black pepper

2 cups heavy cream

2 cups half and half

1 cup fresh or frozen baby peas

½ pound salted butter

1½ pounds dried bucatini pasta

4 ounces freshly grated Parmesan cheese

2 to 3 sprigs fresh parsley, finely chopped

1. Preheat the oven to 375°F. Roast the corn in the husks for 20 minutes. Remove the corn from the oven and, when cool enough to handle, husk the ears and slice the kernels from the cob. Set aside.

2. While the corn is roasting, bring a wide deep skillet of water to a boil. Reduce the heat to a steady simmer. Very gently so as not to break the whites, add the eggs, one at a time, to the simmering water, allowing the water to come back to a simmer after each addition. Have a large bowl of cool water at the ready.

3. Cook the eggs until the whites are firm, but the yolks still quite soft. Scoop them out with a slotted spoon and place them in the bowl of cool water. Set aside.

4. Place the lobster meat in a small bowl and stir in the lemon juice. Cover and chill in the refrigerator.

5. In a cast-iron skillet over medium heat, cook the bacon (or pancetta) until crisp. Remove from the pan, blot with a paper towel to remove excess fat,

and then crumble or chop into a ¼-inch dice. Set aside.

6. In the same skillet, after wiping out most of the bacon grease with a paper towel, cook the onion, garlic, thyme leaves, bay leaves, and pepper until very soft. Remove bay leaves and purée the mixture in a blender.

7. Scrape the onion mixture back into skillet. Add the heavy cream and half and half, cooked bacon, corn kernels, and peas. Simmer the sauce until heated through.

8. Melt the butter, add the lobster with the lemon juice, and heat gently just until warm. Fold into the cream mixture.

9. Cook the bucatini according to the directions on the package. Drain and rinse with fresh, cold water, then add it to the sauce.

10. Divide the pasta and sauce between 8 plates, top each with a poached egg, a generous sprinkle of grated Parmesan, and a pinch or two of chopped parsley.

Tip: You can complete steps 1 to 3 several hours, or even an entire day, ahead of time. Just store everything in the refrigerator. You will need to heat up your poached eggs, of course. To do this, simply heat a pan of water until it just starts to steam. Remove it from the heat and add the chilled eggs with a slotted spoon. Set aside until you are ready to serve dinner.

BROWNE TRADING COMPANY
PORTLAND

Rod Browne Mitchell started selling seafood from the back of a pick-up down by the wharves in the Old Port nearly 30 years ago. A natural entrepreneur with a passion for good food and wine, Rod's start-up found fertile ground on Commercial Street and Browne Trading Company took root on Portland's working waterfront.

Three decades later, the company has grown to an eclectic, diversified enterprise, which is as much a reflection of its founder's love of quality food as it is a response to the city's increasingly sophisticated culinary tastes.

Browne Trading Company boasts a fresh fish and gourmet grocery market and an extensive wine shop, heavy on burgundy and champagne.

Their world class on-site smokehouse produces a variety of expertly smoked seafood, as well as their signature Scotch Cold Smoked Salmon. And the market is also the only company in the United States to co-brand with select caviar farms abroad, supplying caviar to some of the best restaurants and chefs in the country.

Grilled Halibut with Spiced Butter Sauce and Snow Peas

SERVES 2

Fishermen enjoy a short recreational halibut season in May and June in Maine state waters. Hooked lines are set from a tub trawl—usually from lobster boats—similar to longlining. Only five fish are allowed per vessel per year as the species recovers from overfishing.

Firm-fleshed yet delicately flavored, halibut is a natural candidate for grilling. The achiote butter adds color and just enough spice to heighten the spring flavors in this dish.

1 pound filleted halibut, cut into 2 pieces

1 tablespoon olive oil

Sea salt, to taste

Freshly ground black pepper, to taste

1 tablespoon finely chopped fresh parsley

3 cups fresh snow peas, rinsed and trimmed

⅓ cup fish stock (light chicken stock will also work here)

3 tablespoons Spiced Achiote Butter (page 212), cut into cubes and chilled

Watercress, for garnish (optional)

1. Set up the grill for direct grilling and heat it to high.

2. Rinse the halibut under cold running water and pat dry with paper towels. Brush both sides of the fillets with olive oil and season with salt and pepper. Sprinkle chopped parsley on both sides of the fish.

3. Place the fillets in a grill basket or on a fish grate and place on the hot grill. Grill for 4 to 6 minutes on each side, or until cooked through.

4. Meanwhile, cook the snow peas in boiling salted water for about 4 minutes, or until crisp-tender. Drain immediately and rinse with cool water to stop the cooking.

5. In a small saucepan bring the fish stock to a boil. Remove the pan from the heat and whisk in the Spiced Achiote Butter, cube by cube, until the sauce is smooth and satiny.

6. Divide the halibut and snow peas between two plates. Spoon the chili butter sauce over the fish. Garnish with watercress, if desired, and serve.

Oven-Fried Breaded Haddock with Tartar Sauce

SERVES 4

Haddock, the ubiquitous flaky white fish featured on restaurant menus and clam shacks statewide, is fished year-round in Maine. It is readily available fresh or frozen, and is the standard choice for fish sandwiches or a platter of fish and chips.

For a fried fish supper that isn't really fried, this recipe delivers! Crispy on the outside, perfectly tender on the inside, it can be put together fairly quickly to make a weeknight feel like a Friday Fish-Fry.

Tartar Sauce

1 cup mayonnaise

2 tablespoons finely chopped capers

1 tablespoon chopped fresh dill

Juice of 1 medium lemon

Haddock

4 tablespoons unsalted butter

4 cups fresh fine white bread crumbs

1 cup all-purpose flour

2 teaspoons finely chopped fresh parsley

Sea salt and freshly ground black pepper

2 large eggs, beaten

1 pound filleted haddock or cod, cut into 4 pieces

Lemon wedges, for serving

1. Preheat the oven to 400°F.

2. To make the tartar sauce, mix together the mayonnaise, capers, dill, and lemon juice. Season the sauce to taste with salt and pepper and set it aside.

3. To make the haddock, melt the butter over medium-low heat in a wide skillet. Add the bread crumbs and cook gently until they just begin to brown. Scrape them onto some paper towels to blot off the excess fat and then transfer them to a large plate.

4. In a small bowl, mix the flour with the chopped parsley, salt, and pepper. Transfer the mixture to a plate. Place the beaten eggs in a shallow dish, such as a pie pan.

5. Dredge the fish fillets in the seasoned flour, then dip in the egg and finally in the bread crumbs to coat.

6. Place the breaded fish pieces onto a lightly greased sheet pan and bake for 15 to 20 minutes, or until the fish is just cooked through and flakes easily. Serve the fish with the tartar sauce and garnish with lemon wedges.

UNION AT THE PRESS HOTEL

PORTLAND

When Marriott asked Josh Berry to be the executive chef at the restaurant in their new hotel in Portland, he confessed that he wasn't thrilled with the idea of heading up a hotel restaurant.

"There's a stigma," the Maine native says. "I was seeing all these Marriott-approved menus—one meat, one fish, one poultry—and it wasn't working for me."

So Josh asked the advice of a fellow chef and good friend. Standing in the middle of the hotel restaurant, which was under construction at the time, the friend said, "I've got a restaurant for you. It'll be exactly what you want."

"Where?" Josh asked.

"You're standing in it," his friend said. "Make this place your own."

UNION, a seasonally inspired restaurant at the Press Hotel, opened in 2015 with Josh at the helm. The culinary program at UNION is driven primarily by seafood and produce sourced from Portland's working waterfront and nearby farms.

A graduate from the acclaimed apprenticeship program at The Balsams Grand Hotel in New Hampshire, Josh went on to train in Switzerland and Italy before he was ready to commit to a career-track job.

"The goal was always to come back to Maine," Josh recounts, citing northern New England's four distinct seasons as a big draw for his culinary creativity.

Josh credits Maine's short growing season for inspiring his menus at UNION with bursts of varied produce. The menu at the restaurant turns over completely four times a year.

"I think that's what makes this restaurant fun," Josh says. "We're not held by red tape. It's totally different from the typical hotel restaurant."

Outgoing and chatty, Josh enjoys building relationships with the farmers twice a week at the Portland Farmers' Market.

"I need to know the story," Josh admits. "'Cause for me, the story is what it's all about."

Having face-to-face relationships with farmers and fishermen helps him stay connected to the food and what went into growing or catching it, something that he feels is lacking in the modern culture of celebrity chefs.

"When I get a new chef in my kitchen, I ask them to give the fish a name before they start breaking it down," Josh explains. "Because they're going to care more about Jerry or Nancy than they would about 'just some fish.'"

According to Josh, those types of connections contribute to a diner's overall experience.

"Think about the best meal you've ever had, and then think about the most memorable meal you ever had," Josh says. "The two are totally different."

Josh wants guests at UNION to remember their meal there, and he feels that a big part of that is talking to them about how their dinner got to their plate.

UNION's Pan-Seared Local Hake with Littleneck Clams, Bok Choy, Chinese-Fermented Sausage, and Soy Brown Butter

SERVES 2

There are only a few items on UNION's menu that never come off, and this is one of them. Josh will substitute cod for the hake and swap out the vegetables for others in season, but the dish is a perennial favorite among UNION's regular clientele.

Hake, an East Coast deepwater fish that ventures inshore during the warmer months, is having its moment on local restaurant menus. Flakier and more delicate than haddock or cod, hake must be purchased locally and as fresh as possible.

1 tablespoon olive oil

12 ounces hake fillet, cut into 4 pieces

Sea salt

Freshly ground black pepper

⅛ cup Wondra flour

3 tablespoons chilled butter, cut into cubes

1 shallot, thinly sliced

1 tablespoon minced garlic

¼ cup Chinese-fermented sausage, thinly sliced (see Tip)

3 heads baby bok choy, halved and cleaned

8 littleneck clams, scrubbed, rinsed, and patted dry

2 tablespoons soy sauce

½ cup water

2 tablespoons chopped cilantro

1 lemon, halved

1. Preheat the oven to 350°F.

2. Heat a large sauté pan over medium heat, add the olive oil and swirl to evenly coat the bottom of the pan. Season the hake pieces with salt and pepper, then dust it with the flour.

3. Gently place the fish pieces in the hot pan. Drop in the butter and swirl around the fish until brown. Flip the fish once it's golden brown, and cook for 1 to 2 minutes. Place the fish on a baking pan and place in the oven for 7 to 10 minutes, or until just cooked through.

4. While the fish is in the oven, add the shallot, garlic, sausage, bok choy, and clams to the pan of the brown butter. Stir the ingredients until they "get to know each other," as Josh says, or until they are uniformly mixed.

5. Deglaze the pan with the soy sauce and the water. Cover the pan and cook until the clams are open. Taste the broth and adjust seasoning if needed.

6. To serve, divide the ingredients in the pan between two bowls. Top with two pieces of the seared hake and garnish with chopped cilantro and a generous squeeze from the lemon halves.

Tip: You can find Chinese fermented sausage, or "lap cheong," at most Asian grocers. The most common brand in the United States is Kam Yen Jan.

FROM THE FOREST AND THE HIVE

The forest has much to offer for the Maine chef, especially in the way of foraged ingredients. Whether it's mushrooms or fiddleheads, Mainers are well-supplied with unique ingredients to craft specialty dishes original to the Pine Tree State. And of course, everyone's favorite sweeteners, maple syrup and honey, are sourced from Maine forests and hives. The options for forest flavors are truly endless.

The state is also renowned for its game. A coveted destination for visiting hunters and residents alike, Maine's hunting and inland fishing traditions are alive and well. Maine has seasons for dozens of game animals, including deer, wild turkey, rabbit, and moose. Inland fishing includes salmon, bass, several species of trout, and many others.

Cooking wild fish and game—and cooking it well—is a point of pride for hunters and fishermen, and most will have a special recipe they are locally famous for. These dishes may also include wild foraged delicacies such as fiddlehead ferns and edible mushrooms that thrive during their short seasons in Maine's dense forests.

For outdoor sportsmen who want to help their neighbors in need, Hunters for the Hungry—a state program created in 1996—provides an opportunity for hunters to donate harvests to food pantries, soup kitchens, and shelters affiliated with The Emergency Food Assistance Program.

Sautéed Wild Mushrooms with Thyme

SERVES 4

While there is a deep tradition of mushroom foraging in Maine, you don't need to be an expert to acquire and cook with coveted wild varieties. Wild mushroom farming has taken off in the state, and dozens of varieties can be found in the produce department of most grocery stores.

Alternatively, fungi-loving cooks can grow their own mushrooms with the help of home-growing kits from companies like North Spore in Westbrook.

This easy but deeply flavorful appetizer relies on a variety of fresh wild mushrooms.

2 tablespoons olive oil

1 pound mixed wild mushrooms, cleaned, larger mushrooms sliced

Sea salt, to taste

1 tablespoon unsalted butter

2 cloves garlic, finely chopped

3 fresh thyme sprigs, leaves removed from stems

Freshly ground black pepper, to taste

1. Heat the olive oil in a large skillet or cast-iron pan set over a moderate heat. Add the mushrooms and a generous pinch of salt, and sauté until softened and starting to release their juices, 4 to 5 minutes.

2. Add the butter to skillet, let it melt, and then stir in garlic and half the thyme leaves. Continue to sauté for 3 to 4 minutes, or until mushrooms are golden, just starting to crisp, and very tender.

3. Remove from the heat and season to taste with salt and pepper. Garnish with remaining thyme.

NORTH SPORE

WESTBROOK

It's hard for even the most steadfast mushroom despiser to walk away from the North Spore mushroom lab in Westbrook without falling head over heels in love with the funky fungi kingdom within. Led by a charismatic trio of college friends, North Spore cultivates a wide variety of mushrooms for both medicinal uses and the production of spawn (the living genetic material used to grow mushrooms). The growing company does brisk business with their popular home mushroom-growing kits and also produces spawn for commercial growers of culinary-use wild mushrooms.

Most of the company's spawn cultures were grown from mushrooms the crew foraged in the forests of northern New England.

Outside of the North Spore's evolving grow-at-home and medicinal product line, it is clear that their primary mission is sharing their enthusiasm for the mycological world. Made up of a loyal team of brainy millennials, the company is committed to a free-flow of information and knowledge between themselves and their customers.

Mushroom Soup with Chanterelles

SERVES 4

A few days after a soaking rain in the late summer or fall, Maine mushroom foragers will take to the woods to gather just-sprouted fungi from secret spots they've discovered over the years. Most prized of these wild delicacies are the golden, delicately flavored chanterelles, found sprouting in brightly terraced bunches from the damp forest floor. On a good year, foragers will sell their bounty to local restaurants and food co-ops, making them available to the general consumer.

2 tablespoons olive oil

2 shallots, finely chopped

2 cloves garlic, minced

4 cups (about 11 ounces) white button
    mushrooms, brushed clean and diced

½ teaspoon dried thyme

Sea salt

3 cups vegetable stock

⅔ cup heavy cream

2 teaspoons dry sherry

Freshly ground black pepper, to taste

2 tablespoons unsalted butter

2 cups (about 5 ounces) mixed
    chanterelles, brushed clean

6 thyme sprigs, leaves removed from stems

1. Heat the olive oil in a large saucepan set over a medium heat.

2. Add the shallots, garlic, diced mushrooms, dried thyme, and a little sea salt. Sweat the vegetables for 7 to 8 minutes, stirring occasionally.

3. Pour in the stock and simmer for 15 minutes.

4. Puree the soup with an immersion blender until smooth. Stir in the cream and sherry. Season to taste with salt and pepper and keep the soup warm.

5. Meanwhile, melt the butter in a cast-iron skillet set over a moderate heat until the foaming subsides.

6. Add the chanterelles, a little sea salt, and half the fresh thyme leaves, and sauté for 4 to 5 minutes, or until golden and tender.

7. Ladle the soup into bowls and spoon in the chanterelles and garnish with the remaining fresh thyme leaves.

Wild Rabbit Stew with Carrots and Herbs

SERVES 4

Though rabbits are farmed commercially in the state, Mainers can hunt snowshoe hare from the end of September through the end of March. Wild rabbits are best eaten in long-cooked stews to ensure tender meat.

1 rabbit, jointed with liver discarded (see Tip)

3 to 4 tablespoons all-purpose flour

Sea salt, to taste

Freshly ground black pepper, to taste

2 tablespoons sunflower or canola oil

2 tablespoons unsalted butter

3 celery stalks, sliced

5 small to medium carrots, peeled

1 pound pearl onions, peeled and trimmed

1 turnip, peeled and cut into chunks

4 cloves garlic, crushed

1 cup dry white wine

4 fresh thyme sprigs

2 bay leaves

3 cups chicken broth

1 large handful fresh chervil, roughly chopped

1. Preheat the oven to 350°F. Cut the rabbit loin (saddle) into even pieces.

2. Dust the rabbit pieces with flour, shaking off excess. Season generously with salt and pepper.

3. Heat the oil in a large enameled casserole or pot set over a moderate heat. Working in batches, brown the rabbit pieces in the hot oil. Transfer the browned pieces to a plate.

4. Reduce the heat to medium and add the butter to the pot. Stir in celery, carrots, pearl onions, turnip, garlic, and a generous pinch of salt. Sweat the vegetables until softened, about 10 minutes.

5. Increase the heat to moderate and deglaze the pan with the white wine, letting it reduce by two-thirds.

6. Return the rabbit—and any accumulated juices—to the pan, along with the thyme, bay leaves, and broth. Stir well.

7. Bring the stew to a boil and transfer the pot to the oven. Cook, uncovered, until the rabbit is coming away from bone and vegetables are very tender to the tip of a knife, about 1 hour.

8. Remove from the oven and season stew with salt and pepper to taste. Sprinkle over chervil before serving.

Tip: Ask your butcher to joint your rabbit into rear and front legs, loin (saddle), and belly.

TOPS'L FARM

WALDOBORO

Tops'l Farm isn't your typical farm. There aren't tilled rows of beets and kale and cabbage as far as the eye can see. Instead, there are soft, wild fields and misty forests surrounding an Ewok-like village of linen-colored canvas tents and rustic A-frame cabins furnished with vintage camp beds and Pendleton wool blankets.

A gentle, rolling one-and-a-half-mile hike from the campground leads to the estuarial shores of Medomak River and the unlikely venue for the farm's unique culinary program.

Inspired by their off-the-beaten-path adventures at home and abroad, Tops'l Farm owners Sarah and Josh Pike wanted to create unique lodgings and culinary experiences that tapped into the adventurer's sense of discovery.

Each season the farm hosts a series of seasonally inspired, hyper-local dinners at long tables under the trees or inside a wood and canvas yurt overlooking the river. A rustic outdoor bar is decked with lights and candles, and Adirondack chairs—each equipped with a warm wool blanket and a cozy sheep's fleece—encircle a stone fire pit crackling with glowing logs.

"I wanted to create an experience for people; give them that element of surprise and delight,"

Sarah explains about the design of the space, and how it echoes her own best culinary experiences.

Six times a year, Sarah invites a different chef to create an evening meal that captures what she calls "the four seasonal culinary expressions of Maine."

Three of these meals take place in the summer and celebrate the bounty of the Medomak River. Guests enjoy a five-course river- and forest-inspired meal at a long communal table on the riverbank. Courses feature beer pairings from local breweries, and Sarah, acting as bartender, supplies guests with her signature cocktails made from wild-foraged plants.

Fall brings the farm's annual Wild Game & Wine Dinner and an opportunity for diners to experience true wild Maine game the way it was meant to be experienced—cooked outdoors over an open fire. The actual meal takes place in the yurt and each of the five courses are paired with natural and biodynamic wines.

In the winter, Sarah and her team invite guests to strap on their snowshoes and hike out to an atmospheric Swiss-inspired meal in the riverside yurt. And the short but sweet springtime sugaring season gives guests an opportunity to shake off the winter with warm cocktails and a five-course Maine maple dinner in the farm's post-and-beam event barn.

Sarah, who grew up on a homestead MOFGA-certified beef farm in mid-coast Maine, says these kinds of events would have been so helpful for her family and the farmers she grew up with. Her deep appreciation for the work of farmers, and her

enthusiasm for sustainable food systems, runs like a current through each of the farm's culinary events.

"My job," she says, "is to pull the talents of all these passionate people together and sprinkle a little fairy dust on it."

Moose Bourguignon

SERVES 4 TO 6 PEOPLE

In Maine, there is a short but coveted hunting season for moose. Permits are applied for with excitement and issued by a lottery drawing that occurs at the end of June. In 2019, just under 3,000 permits were issued. Hunters are limited to one moose per permit.

According to chef Ken Burkett, his recipe for Moose Bourguignon is a perfect remedy for a gloomy, cold, late-fall day. As in hunting, patience is the key in braising game meat. This recipe will allow you to cook the moose to the required tenderness without overcooking your vegetables.

15 baby carrots, peeled

1 pound red pearl onions, peeled

Kosher salt and ground black pepper, to taste

1 tablespoon olive oil

8 ounce pork belly or thick-cut bacon,
    cut into lardons (¼-inch cubes)

3 pounds moose chuck, cut into 2-inch cubes

1 pound button mushroom, quartered

3 tablespoons tomato paste

4 cloves garlic, roughly chopped

8 ounces unsalted butter

1 cup all-purpose flour

1 bottle (750-milliliter) red wine—
    use what you like to drink

4 cups beef stock

3 fresh or dried bay leaves

2 tablespoons chopped fresh thyme leaves

2 cups parsley leaves, for garnish

1 fresh baguette, for serving

1. Preheat the oven to 400°F. Season carrots and onions with salt and pepper, spread them onto a sheet pan, and place them in the oven. Cook until the carrots are slightly browned, about 10 minutes. Onions will be caramelized. Set aside.

2. In a large Dutch oven over medium-high heat, heat the olive oil until shimmering. Add the bacon and cook, stirring occasionally, until the bacon is lightly browned, about 10 minutes. Remove the bacon with a slotted spoon to a large plate.

3. Pat dry the moose cubes with paper towels and season liberally with salt and pepper. In the same pot in which you cooked the bacon, sear the moose in batches of single layers for 3 to 5 minutes, turning to brown on all sides. Leave plenty of room between the cubes of meat to promote browning on the meat rather than steaming.

4. Remove the seared moose to the plate with the bacon. Set aside.

5. In the same pot, add all of the mushrooms. Cook the mushrooms until all their liquid is evaporated and they begin to brown.

6. Add the tomato paste and garlic to the pot with the mushrooms. Cook and continue to stir until fragrant for 3 to 5 minutes. Add 4 ounces of the butter and all of the flour, stirring constantly. Cook this roux for another 3 to 5 minutes, making sure to scrape the bottom of the pan.

7. Add the wine and beef stock and bring the stew to a boil, stirring frequently.

8. Reduce the heat to a low simmer and stir in the bacon, moose, and bay leaves. Cover the pot and cook until the moose is fork tender (will slide off fork with ease), about 1 hour.

9. Finish the dish with chopped thyme leaves and season to taste with salt and pepper.

10. To serve, ladle the finished stew into bowls, evenly distributing the carrots and onion. Garnish with the parsley. The stew is best eaten with toasted baguette slices and good butter.

Honey-Glazed Sweet Potatoes and Squash with Chile and Halloumi

SERVES 6

While commercial beekeepers play a requisite role in Maine's agricultural industry by providing pollination services, beekeeping has also become a popular pastime with hobbyists. Restaurants like UNION in Portland even keep their own rooftop hives and feature their raw honey and comb in an array of striking and unusual dishes. In this savory side dish, the vegetables are coated in a slightly spicy dressing of honey and olive oil, which caramelizes into a deep golden brown.

1 small butternut squash, peeled, seeded, and cut into ½-inch cubes

2 large sweet potatoes, peeled and cut into 2-inch wedges

3 tablespoons olive oil

2 tablespoons honey

1 small red jalapeño, sliced

¼ cup pumpkin seeds

2 tablespoons sesame seeds

Sea salt, to taste

Freshly ground black pepper, to taste

8 ounces halloumi, cubed

5 to 6 fresh basil leaves, finely julienned

1. Preheat the oven to 375°F. Toss the squash and sweet potatoes with the olive oil, honey, jalapeño, pumpkin seeds, sesame seeds, salt, and pepper in a large bowl. Spill the vegetables onto a pan and cook in the oven for 30 minutes.

2. Remove the pan from the oven and add the cubed halloumi to the pan. Stir gently to mix the cheese in with the vegetables.

3. Pop the pan back into the oven and roast for another 20 to 30 minutes, or until everything is golden brown and the vegetables are tender.

4. Remove the pan from the oven and transfer the vegetables to a serving plate. Scatter the dish with the sliced basil and serve.

SWAN'S HONEY

ALBION

Growing food for a living is a high-risk business. It's dependent on a fair amount of things that are, for the most part, out of the farmer's control—weather, market demand, good health, and pollination.

When Karen and Lincoln Sennett gave up their careers in other states to move back home and take over their family's wild blueberry business, they saw an opportunity to lower the stakes for farmers like themselves by making pollination less of a wild card.

In 2002, the couple bought a well-respected honey and bee business in Brewer and moved the hives to their early 19th-century family farm in Albion. They grew the hives from several hundred to several thousand, and now, not only produce a varied line of honeys and bee products,

but also provide much-needed pollination services on farms throughout Maine and Georgia. They also offer educational programs, private label products, nucs (starter hives created from a larger colony), and beekeeping equipment.

Swan's produces at least eight different kinds of honey, including several mono-floral varieties including buckwheat, wild blueberry, wild raspberry, tupelo, gallberry, and orange blossom.

Maple Baked Beans

SERVES 4

There are many reasons to celebrate a Maine spring, not the least of which is sugaring season. Take a chilly stroll down any country road in March and you'll find sap buckets hanging from bare-branched maples, collecting raw watery sap drop by drop. Go a few miles inland or to the northern forests close to the Canadian border and you'll find hundreds of miles of tap lines weaving in and out of dense woods, eventually heading downhill to a central collection station.

Baked beans are a traditional New England cold-weather supper usually made with molasses. This version substitutes a generous amount of maple syrup for part of the molasses, creating a distinctly northern variation.

1½ cups dried Great Northern beans, rinsed
    and soaked overnight in cold water

4 ounces roughly chopped thick-sliced bacon

1 cup water

1 cup maple syrup

2 small white onions, chopped

2½ tablespoons tomato ketchup

2½ tablespoons molasses

1½ tablespoons apple cider vinegar

2 teaspoons Dijon or wholegrain mustard

½ teaspoon Worcestershire sauce

Freshly ground black pepper, to taste

Sea salt, to taste

1. Preheat the oven to 350°F.

2. Drain the soaked beans and place them in an enameled oven-proof soup pot or cast-iron kettle with the bacon, water, maple syrup, onions, ketchup, molasses, vinegar, mustard, Worcestershire sauce, and black pepper to taste.

3. Stir thoroughly to combine before covering dish with an oven-proof lid or aluminum foil.

4. Transfer the pot to the oven and bake, stirring once or twice during the cooking time, until beans are tender and sauce has thickened, about 1 hour.

5. When the beans are quite tender, remove the pot from the oven and stir in salt to taste.

6. Serve the warm, saucy beans with Brown Bread (page 32) and plenty of good butter.

STRAWBERRY HILL FARMS
SKOWHEGAN

The Steeves family, fourth- and fifth-generation maple producers, have been tapping maple trees and bottling MOFGA-certified organic maple syrup for sale since the 1840s. Today, the farm operates 40,000 of the 1¼ million taps in Somerset County, the largest maple-producing county in the nation.

Jack Steeves, in his 80s, along with wife, Eva, and son, Jeremy, own and operate Strawberry Hill Farm, and are one of the eight Maine maple producers who created the almost 40-year-old Maine Maple Sunday tradition, celebrated annually on the 4th Sunday in March.

The celebration, created to promote Maine maple products, is a day that the general public can visit participating farms to observe and learn about tapping trees, collecting sap, and the intensive evaporation process necessary to convert sap into syrup at a staggering ratio of 40 parts sap to one part syrup. Visitors can also taste-test dozens of maple products and foods made with maple syrup at each farm—treats like traditional snow-frozen maple taffy, maple caramel corn, fresh maple doughnuts, and even maple ice cream.

The annual celebration that started in 1983 with just a few farms participating, now includes over 80 maple producers from Northern to Southern Maine and has even spread outside the state as far west as Ohio.

Maine Maple Sunday is so popular, in fact, that some producers sell their entire season's production on that single day.

Strawberry Hill Farms has over 3,500 visitors on that Sunday in March, and the Steeveses see it as an opportunity to promote the sale of their syrup—about 12,000 gallons annually—year round.

Spaghetti with Fiddleheads and Artichokes

SERVES 4

Fiddleheads, the just-sprouted unfurled head of the Ostrich fern, are a much-anticipated wild-foraged food all over Maine. They are only available for a couple of weeks in the spring, and will appear at farmers' markets and grocery stores. The ferns taste a little like if asparagus married broccoli, and they must be cooked to be edible. In this simple pasta dish, they add texture and interest—as well as complementary flavor—to crisp asparagus and tender baby artichokes.

1 pound dried spaghetti

¼ cup olive oil

3 cloves garlic, finely chopped

½ cup asparagus tips, blanched

1 pound fresh baby artichokes, trimmed and blanched, then quartered

½ cup fresh fiddleheads, cleaned and blanched

Sea salt, to taste

Freshly ground black pepper, to taste

½ cup grated Parmesan

1. Cook pasta until al dente. Drain, rinse, and set aside.

2. Meanwhile, heat olive oil and garlic in a large skillet over medium-high heat. Add the asparagus, artichokes, and fiddleheads and sauté until they just begin to crisp.

3. Add cooked and drained pasta to the skillet and stir gently to mix everything together; you may want to use tongs for this. Season with salt and pepper. Garnish with Parmesan to serve.

Halibut with Chanterelles

SERVES 4

One magical spring at the tail end of Maine's short halibut season, a friend brought me an early-foraged harvest of wild chanterelles. Both delicately flavored, the dense white fish and the striking orange-colored mushrooms are a perfectly paired match for an unusual and celebratory spring meal.

3 tablespoons olive oil

1½ cups Israeli couscous

2¼ cups vegetable broth or water

4 halibut fillets, skin and pin bones removed

Sea salt, to taste

¼ teaspoon freshly ground mixed peppercorns

2 tablespoons unsalted butter, cubed

6 ounces chanterelle mushrooms, cleaned

Freshly ground black pepper, to taste

1 tablespoon chopped fresh thyme leaves

1. Heat 1 tablespoon of the olive oil in a Dutch oven or large saucepan set over a moderate heat.

2. Add the couscous and sauté until toasted, stirring frequently, 3 to 4 minutes. Stir in the broth or water and bring to a boil. Once boiling, reduce the heat to low and cover with a lid, cooking until the couscous has absorbed the broth and is tender to the bite, 15 to 20 minutes.

3. In the meantime, season the halibut fillets with some salt and ground mixed peppercorns.

4. Heat 1 tablespoon oil in a cast-iron skillet set over a medium heat. Place the halibut in the skillet, and cook until the flesh is bright white and opaque, 6 to 8 minutes.

5. Carefully flip and cook the other sides until the flesh is golden, 1 to 2 minutes. Remove the halibut to a plate and cover with foil to keep warm.

6. Set the pan back over a moderate heat and add the remaining oil and then the butter, letting it melt.

7. Once melted, add the mushrooms and a pinch of salt, sautéing until they have released their juices and are golden brown, 5 to 6 minutes. Remove the skillet from the heat and season the mushrooms to taste with salt and pepper.

8. When ready, drain the couscous if needed and divide between 4 plates. Set the halibut fillets on top and spoon over the mushrooms. Scatter with the fresh thyme and serve.

Tagliatelle with Porcini and Parmesan Sauce

SERVES 4

Large, densely fleshed porcini mushrooms can be found in damp autumn woods and, because of their large size, are often dried for later use. Here they add their distinct woodsy flavor to salty pancetta and sweet cream, balancing everything for this soothing and satisfying dish.

1 pound dried tagliatelle

2 tablespoon olive oil

5 ounces chopped pancetta

8 ounces fresh roughly sliced porcini mushrooms

Sea salt, to taste

½ cup dry white wine

1 cup heavy cream

½ cup Parmesan, finely grated, plus extra for serving

Freshly ground black pepper, to taste

1 small handful flat-leaf parsley, chopped

1. Cook the tagliatelle in a large saucepan of salted, boiling water until al dente, 8 to 10 minutes.

2. Meanwhile, heat the olive oil in a large sauté pan set over a moderate heat until hot. Add the pancetta and sauté for 3 to 4 minutes until golden brown.

3. Add the mushrooms and a large pinch of salt, and sauté for another 3 to 4 minutes until tender and lightly golden.

4. Add the wine and let it reduce by three-quarters. Drain the pasta at this point, reserving 1 cup of the starchy cooking liquid.

5. Add the cream and Parmesan to the mushrooms, stirring well to combine. Bring to a simmer and then add the pasta and a little of the starchy cooking liquid.

6. Stir well and continue to cook for 2 to 3 minutes until the pasta clings to the thickened sauce, adding more of the cooking liquid as needed. Season to taste with salt and pepper.

7. Spoon the pasta and sauce into bowls. Top with chopped parsley, some freshly ground black pepper, and serve with grated Parmesan on the side for sprinkling over.

MICMAC FARMS

CARIBOU

When native brook trout started manifesting environmental mercury from the rivers and streams of northern Maine, the Aroostook Band of Micmacs took measures to protect this traditional tribal food by developing a plan to farm the fish on land.

After seven years of fundraising and construction, the Micmac Fish Farm started raising native brook trout in 2015, in a 34,000-gallon aquaculture facility located at Micmac Farms in Caribou. The facility provides fresh brook trout to the tribal community as well as the general public by selling the fish at their on-site 2,700-square-foot farmers' market, off-site farmers' markets, and fresh fish markets in Rockland, Portland, and Portsmouth, New Hampshire. The farm also delivers live fish to ponds throughout Maine.

Micmac Farms began as a community garden in 2009. Today, the farm cultivates four acres of perennial orchards, two acres of native pollinator habitat, and two acres of seasonal produce. Their facility includes processing space, greenhouses, plus the hatchery and farmers' market.

The produce and the fish raised at Micmac Farms are harvested the same day they're offered for sale, ensuring that the farmers' mission of creating direct access to good food in tribal lands is being met. The farm is committed to sustainable farming practices and providing support for other tribal entrepreneurs.

Everything Micmac Farms brings to market is certified "Made/Produced by American Indians," and, in the coming years, the farm hopes to increase its presence in wider markets with the introduction of value-added products.

Honey- and Soy-Glazed Brook Trout

SERVES 4

The brook trout raised at Micmac Farms are hatched from native Maine brook trout eggs acquired from the Enfield Fish Hatchery. The farm does not breed its own stock, as it is important to the tribe that the fish are genetically the same as wild trout. The Micmac trout, however, have a distinctive bright pink flesh, rather than the more typical white, due to the diet of freshwater shrimp, earthworms, and soy protein they are fed on the farm.

2 tablespoons honey

¼ cup dark soy sauce

2 large brook trout fillets, pin-bones removed

2 tablespoons canola oil

8 ounces green beans, trimmed

Sea salt, to taste

Freshly ground black pepper, to taste

1 lime, cut in half

2 tablespoons toasted sesame seeds

1. Preheat the oven to 400°F. Whisk together the honey and soy sauce in a small bowl until the honey dissolves.

2. Arrange the trout fillets on a baking sheet lined with parchment paper and brush with about half the glaze. Season with a little black pepper.

3. Roast the fish until opaque and firm to the touch with a slight spring, 10 to 12 minutes.

4. In the meantime, heat the oil in a large skillet or wok; if using a wok, preheat it before adding the oil and swirling to coat the surface.

5. Add the green beans and a pinch of salt and pepper, stir-frying for 2 minutes. Cover with a lid and steam over a reduced heat until tender to the bite, 2 to 3 minutes.

6. Remove the lid and set off the heat until ready to serve. Remove the trout from the oven when ready.

7. Transfer the trout and beans to a serving platter. Spoon over the remaining glaze and squeeze over some lime juice. Sprinkle with toasted sesame seeds and serve straight away.

Roasted Venison Loin with Herbs and Spices

SERVES 6

If a deer hunter ever gifts you with fresh venison, it will most likely be a portion of the tenderloin, as this is the easiest for the uninitiated to cook. If cooked to medium rare, this dish produces a smooth, tender, and flavorful roast suitable for company.

4 pounds venison tenderloin roast

6 slices bacon

1 cup beef consommé

1 cup red wine

11 teaspoons fresh lemon juice

2 cloves garlic, finely chopped

1 small onion, finely chopped

Sea salt, to taste

Fresh coarsely ground black pepper, to taste

1 teaspoon fresh finely chopped thyme leaves

1 teaspoon fresh finely chopped rosemary leaves

1. Preheat the oven to 500° F.

2. Remove any fat or dry skin from the roast. Rinse roast and pat dry with paper towels. Place in roasting pan and sear in oven for 10 minutes.

3. Reduce heat to 425°F and arrange the bacon slices over the roast. Roast, uncovered, for 30 to 40 minutes. Remove browned bacon slices.

4. In a bowl, whisk consommé, red wine, lemon juice, garlic, onion, salt, pepper, thyme, and rosemary. Pour over roast. Cover roast loosely with aluminum foil and continue roasting until venison is tender (about 20 minutes per pound for medium rare). Baste frequently during the roasting process. I don't recommend roasting beyond medium, as this will toughen the meat.

5. Let the roast rest for about 15 minutes before carving. Garnish with herbs and spices. Serve.

FROM THE CREAMERY

There are over 200 dairy farms in Maine, accounting for over $120 million in annual revenue, second only to potatoes in overall agricultural value.

Maine-produced dairy supplies a growing number of artisanal cheese makers in the state and several growing butter companies.

A whopping 27 percent of Maine's dairies are certified organic—one of the highest percentages in the nation—and yet, most of the organic milk headed for the shelves in major grocery stores is shipped out of state for processing. Maine's only organic processing facility closed in 2014, leaving the state's larger organic dairy producers susceptible to federally mandated dairy prices.

Maine is also home to a growing number of artisanal cheese makers, who use cow, goat, and sheep's milk to make aged, fresh, and soft-ripened cheeses. According to the Maine Cheese Guild, there are over 90 licensed cheese makers in Maine, with new ones popping up every year.

While most homestead Maine dairies make butter from an overabundance of cream in the summertime, only a few of them offer their butters for sale at farmers' markets and small gourmet grocery stores. Maine is lucky enough to have two major award-winning butter producers: Kate's Gourmet Butter, and Casco Bay Creamery.

Home-"Churned" Butter

MAKES APPROXIMATELY 10 OUNCES

The Holmes family at Misty Brook Farm have their own butter churn that they use to convert any surplus cream in the summer to butter that they then freeze for use all winter long. Of course, not everyone has a butter churn, so below is Katia Holmes's simple technique for making butter without a churn.

32 ounces heavy cream

1. Place the cream in a half-gallon jar. With a group of friends, or your family, shake the jar vigorously. When you get tired, pass the jar to the next person.

2. Eventually you will have whipped cream. Keep shaking. In time, the cream will separate into solid bits of butter and buttermilk.

3. Strain the butter through a mesh sieve or cheesecloth. Store the buttermilk in the refrigerator for future baking projects. Press the bits of butter into a block, blot dry, and wrap in butcher paper or butter paper and store in the refrigerator.

Tip: Katia says this method goes slightly faster if the cream is at room temperature.

Spiced Achiote Butter

MAKES ABOUT ½ POUND OF BUTTER

Use this high-spice, high-flavor butter for the El El Frijoles Lobster Tacos recipe on page 174, to spice up a bowl of steamed mussels or clams, or to sauté anything from spinach to fiddleheads.

½ pound butter, softened

3 cloves garlic

1 tablespoon Achiote paste (this can be found at specialty food stores or at a Mexican grocery)

½ teaspoon kosher salt

Juice from 1 lime

½ teaspoon chili powder (or more if you like it spicy)

¼ cup olive oil

1. Place all ingredients except the olive oil in a food processor. Process until smooth.

2. With the processor running, slowly add the olive oil in a thin, steady stream. Blend until smooth.

3. Divide into four portions and store in small, airtight containers in your freezer.

Blue Cheese Sauce

SERVES 4 TO 6

Make this sauce with a crumbly, not-too-dry blue cheese, and serve it alongside grilled steaks, pan-fried polenta, or spicy barbecued chicken wings. You might also want to try it tossed with wide, buttered noodles for a quick, satisfying weeknight supper.

¾ **cup heavy cream**

1 **pound blue cheese**

1 **teaspoon Worcestershire sauce**

1 **teaspoon lemon juice**

¼ **teaspoon sea salt**

¼ **teaspoon freshly ground black pepper**

¼ **cup fresh chopped flat-leaf parsley**

1. Warm the cream to a simmering point in a sauce-pan set over a moderate heat. Simmer steadily until slightly thickened, 4 to 5 minutes.

2. As the cream simmers, crumble about half the blue cheese. Stir the crumbled blue cheese into the cream with a fork, mashing it to remove any larger lumps.

3. Reduce the heat to low and stir in the Worcester-shire sauce, lemon juice, salt, and pepper.

4. Pour the sauce into a serving jug. Serve with the remaining blue cheese on the side, garnished with chopped parsley.

CASCO BAY CREAMERY

SCARBOROUGH

Before mechanical butter churns, industrial-sized mixers, and a varied product line of compound butters and cream cheese, Alicia Menard and Jennell Carter had a stand mixer in a local church kitchen and a dream to make real butter out of fresh Maine cream.

"We start with higher-quality, higher-butterfat cream and milk," says Alicia. "We buy cream from local dairy farmers when available and are proud to support small, family dairy farms."

The growing company also uses locally produced maple syrup and spices for their popular compound butters in flavors like Lemon & Chive, Maple, Garlic & Herb, Blue Cheese, and Truffle.

Today, the couple and their team work out of a dedicated facility in Scarborough, producing butter, cream cheese, and compound butters for a growing wholesale market, local restaurants and food producers, and a loyal customer base who they got to know in their early days while selling at area farmers' markets.

"We continue to be grateful and amazed by the support of our customers," Alicia says. "It's an honor to be in their refrigerators, part of their recipes, and on their dinner tables."

Honey Butter Popcorn

MAKES 12 CUPS

Alicia Menard, co-owner of Casco Bay Creamery, says that one of the ways she and her wife and business partner, Jennell Carter, unwind after a long day at the creamery is to make some buttered popcorn and watch a movie. This is their favorite recipe. The honey adds unexpected sweetness to a classic snack, while the sea salt comes together to tie in every flavor.

12 cups popped popcorn (from ½ cup kernels)
¼ cup unsalted butter, melted
2 to 3 tablespoons honey
¼ teaspoon sea salt

1. Place the popcorn in a large bowl.

2. In a glass measuring cup, mix together the butter and honey. Drizzle the mixture over the popcorn while stirring to coat evenly.

3. Sprinkle the buttered popcorn with salt and serve while still warm.

CROOKED FACE CREAMERY

SKOWHEGAN

Specializing in fresh, whole-milk cheeses since 2010, Amy Rowbottom's Crooked Face Creamery has gained a following in Maine and beyond.

After living out of state and pursuing a career in marketing, Amy returned to her parents' dairy farm in Norridgewock to reevaluate what she wanted to do with her life. She realized that she missed the farm she grew up on and the lifestyle she had as a farm kid in northern Maine. Amy decided that she wanted to give her kids a similar way of life, so she moved back home and got to work figuring out how to make a go of it.

Cheese was a natural progression from her dairy farm roots and Amy found she had a passion for it. When she created her signature product, an applewood-smoked ricotta, she felt she had stumbled onto something special.

Amy has since moved her operation from her parents' farm to her own facility in the Maine Grains gristmill in Skowhegan. Her Up North Applewood Cold Smoked Ricotta continues to be the star of the show, but the creamery has expanded into aged cheeses and cheese spreads. The creamery's products are sold at specialty grocery stores throughout Maine and served at some of the best farm-to-table restaurants in the state.

Strawberry Bruschetta with Ricotta and Arugula

SERVES 8

Use a creamy, dense whole-milk ricotta for this recipe. If you can get Crooked Face Creamery's cold smoked ricotta, you will find that the smoked flavors mingle magically with the fresh fruit and peppery arugula. But even a plain ricotta, so long as it's fresh and creamy, will hold up to the somewhat spicy sweetness of the red fruits and create a dramatic backdrop for their juices.

2 cups fresh hulled and diced strawberries

2 tablespoons pomegranate seeds

Sea salt, to taste

Freshly ground black pepper, to taste

1 baguette

1 cup ricotta cheese

2 cups arugula, washed and chopped
     if the leaves are very large

1. Toss diced strawberries and pomegranate seeds with a pinch of salt and pepper in a mixing bowl. Set aside.

2. Cut baguette, on bias, into at least 8 slices, preferably more.

3. Spread slices with ricotta cheese and top with arugula. Spoon diced strawberries and pomegranate on top before serving.

APPLETON CREAMERY

APPLETON

With a herd of 40 Alpine dairy goats and an organic garden of fresh herbs and "goat treats," Caitlin and Brad Hunter's small-scale farm and dairy in midcoast Maine has been producing award-winning cheeses since 1994.

The creamery specializes primarily in fresh plain and herbed goat cheese (chèvre), but also makes a few aged varieties of both goat and cow cheeses—best known for their Granite Kiss (a soft-ripened goat cheese layered with vegetable ash) and their goat and cow "Camdenbert" (a Camembert-style soft cheese named for the nearby coastal town of Camden). All the cheeses are available at the on-site farm stand, where you can visit with Brad, Caitlin, her sister Megan, or one of the farm's apprentices, taste and buy

cheeses, and say hello to the goats. The creamery crew also attends several farmers' markets year round, and the cheese is carried at a handful of local specialty grocery stores and restaurants.

Beet and Arugula Bruschetta with Chive Goat Cheese Spread

SERVES 4

The following appetizer or light lunch could be prepared any time of year, but is especially celebratory in the spring, just as the first chives burst through the thaw.

Virtually all goat dairies in Maine produce chèvre, a soft, fresh cheese denser than ricotta, but with a pleasant, spreadable consistency. The best chèvre is buttery, with a distinctive sharp tang. Many chèvre makers also offer flavored varieties—much like compound butters—which is essentially what we're doing here with the addition of chives.

4 small beets, about the size of apricots

½ cup shelled pistachios

1 cup soft fresh goat cheese (chèvre)

1 small bunch chives, snipped

2 tablespoons hot water

Sea salt

Freshly ground black pepper

3 cups arugula, washed

Extra virgin olive oil

4 thick slices sourdough bread

1. Preheat the oven to 375°F.

2. Scrub the beets and wrap them loosely in aluminum foil. Place the foil packet on the center rack in the oven and roast for 30 to 45 minutes, or until the

beets are fork tender. Allow the cooked beets to cool completely, then gently rub the skins off and cut them into ¼-inch dice.

3. Toast the pistachios in a dry skillet set over a moderate heat until aromatic and golden. Tip them out onto a cutting board and give them a rough chop.

4. In a small bowl, stir together the goat cheese, chives, hot water, a sprinkle of salt, and a grind of pepper until smooth and spreadable. Add more hot water as needed to reach a spreadable consistency.

5. In a large bowl, toss the arugula, chopped beets, toasted pistachios, and enough olive oil to coat. Add salt and pepper to taste.

6. Toast the bread in a toaster or under a hot broiler. Spread the toast slices thickly with the goat cheese mixture and then cut them in half diagonally.

7. Top each toast with the beet-arugula salad and serve immediately.

BALFOUR FARM

PITTSFIELD

Heather and Doug Donahue began their small-scale farm operation with a couple of chickens in the early 2000s. Both had other careers at the time—contract building and teaching—but as they built their livestock, their own lives began to take a new shape.

Today, the Donahues tend a herd of 12 Normande dairy cows and operate an organic, MOFGA-certified farmstead dairy—one of just a handful in Maine—producing both fresh and aged cheeses and fresh and cultured dairy products. All their aged cheeses are produced with raw milk from their own cows. They are probably best known for their award-winning Haymaker English-style cheddars, which include a striking red-veined variety spiked with ghost pepper salt and ground chipotle chiles and aged in black wax.

The farm boasts a small on-site store—The Little Cheese Shop—which sells not only cheese, but "all things that go with cheese." Maine-made charcuterie, crackers, preserves, beer, and wine fill the shelves, as well as a small supply of baking ingredients.

HAHN'S END

PHIPPSBURG

One of Maine's most celebrated cheese makers has been at her craft for over 20 years. But you won't find her cheeses online and you won't find them outside of Maine. The passionate fans of Deb Hahn's cheeses will instead track a wedge of Blue Velvet or Eleanor's Buttercup to a retail outpost lucky enough to carry it.

Notoriously humble, Deb Hahn crafts aged raw cow's milk cheeses known for their depth of flavor and attractive rinds. City of Ships, named for the nearby shipbuilding town of Bath, is a Comte-style hard cheese with a nutty, buttery flavor that is universally appealing and one of Deb's most popular varieties.

Her cheeses are served at well-known farm-to-table restaurants, at a few specialty grocery stores and co-ops up and down the coast, and by Deb herself at a handful of farmers' markets.

BAKER BROOK FARM

GRAY

The day in 1998 that Alan O'Brien decided to raise a couple dairy heifers for Cumberland County's 4-H Club is the day Baker Brook Farm officially began. His parents, Steve and Diane O'Brien, nurtured their son's early interest in farming by helping him add Holsteins, Ayrshires, and Jerseys to his growing herd.

Alan became an understudy to a herdsman at a local dairy farm, learning animal husbandry and how to milk, care for, and treat a dairy herd.

By 2009, with a herd of 50 cows, Alan became the youngest milk producer for Oakhurst, Maine's largest dairy company.

Today, both Steve and Diane manage the business side of things, while Alan manages the 120-cow herd, milking, and hay production. The company self-distributes Baker Brook Farm–brand milk to colleges, restaurants, coffee houses, and other artisanal food producers throughout southern Maine.

Panna Cotta with Raspberries

SERVES 4

Panna cotta, an Italian eggless custard, is a snap to make as it doesn't require the tempering of eggs and milk. Instead, it relies on gelatin and fresh cream for its delicate and creamy texture. For the best, fullest flavor, use cream that has not been ultra-pasteurized and that is ideally fewer than a few days old. Pasteurization is the technique of heat-treating food products in order to destroy harmful bacteria that may grow to unhealthy amounts over time. Maine is also home to a handful of raw milk producers, most of whom sell directly from their farms. If you happen to live near a homestead dairy farm, hyper fresh raw milk and cream is a full-flavored treat hard to come by in mainstream grocery stores.

Custard

2 tablespoons cold water

1 envelope (about 1 tablespoon) unflavored granulated gelatin

2 cups heavy cream

½ cup half and half

⅓ cup granulated sugar

1½ teaspoons vanilla extract

Raspberry Sauce

1½ cups fresh raspberries

2 tablespoons granulated sugar

1 tablespoon orange juice

1 tablespoon cornstarch

½ cup cold water

1. To make the custard, place the cold water in a small bowl and sprinkle the gelatin over it. Let the mixture stand about 1 minute, then place the bowl over a pan of steaming water and melt the hydrated gelatin.

2. In a large saucepan, bring the cream, half and half, and sugar to a boil, stirring constantly. When the cream mixture boils, immediately remove the pan from the heat and stir in the gelatin mixture and vanilla extract. Divide the mixture between 4 dessert glasses and cool to room temperature. Chill, covered, for at least 4 hours.

3. To make the raspberry sauce, gently wash the raspberries; reserve ½ cup for garnish. In a saucepan over medium-high heat, combine 1 cup raspberries, the sugar, and orange juice.

4. In a small bowl, whisk the cornstarch into the cold water until smooth. Pour the cornstarch mixture into the saucepan and bring to a boil.

5. Reduce the heat and simmer the raspberry mixture for about 5 minutes, stirring frequently. The sauce will continue to thicken as it cools.

6. Puree the sauce with a handheld immersion blender or in a blender. Strain the sauce through a fine strainer or sieve to remove the raspberry seeds.

7. To serve: Drizzle raspberry sauce on or around plated panna cotta. Garnish with fresh raspberries.

FROM THE ORCHARD

It is a gleaming morning, cool and blue. The air is light and heady, having shed summer like a damp beach towel. The sunlight bounces off leaves just turning from dark green to yellow, from red to orange, promising a day of country roads, sweeping fields, and deciduous forests bathed in a crisp, golden glow.

It can only be an autumn morning in Maine. There is an orchard out there waiting for you. Acres of green-leafed apple, pear, and plum trees, laden with fruit in colors that put the maples to shame. Ruby, pink, wine, gold, and reds so dark you'll call them black. There will be baskets to borrow there, and poles with hooks and bags to help you reach the fruit at the very tops of trees, because those are the very best. There will be bakeries at these orchards, fragrant with warm cider doughnuts, bubbling pies, and glazed cakes. There will be barrels upon barrels of already-picked fruit of all varieties. And sometimes, there will even be music.

There will be fields and lawns there, still green and soft as moss, welcoming your blanket, your basket, and your company. And on this sweet, bright morning, there will be time to prepare a meal that you will pack in a basket, or a bag, or a bucket, and then eat outside in the warm afternoon sun.

Sweet Potato Pancakes with Apples and Maple Syrup

SERVES 4

Sweet potato crops, fairly new to Maine farms and gardens, appear in the fall alongside crates of apples and other orchard fruits. Here, they provide a vegan base for a soft, delicately orange pancake, which has the surprise crunch of a slightly caramelized apple in the middle.

¾ cup all-purpose flour

¾ cup spelt flour, or oat flour

3 tablespoons granulated sugar

3 teaspoons baking powder

¼ teaspoon baking soda

½ teaspoon salt

½ teaspoon ground cinnamon

1 cup unsweetened almond milk

3 tablespoons water

⅓ cup cooked, mashed sweet potato

2 tablespoon coconut oil, melted,
    plus extra for frying

3 teaspoons ground flax seed

1 teaspoon apple cider vinegar, or lemon juice

1 teaspoon vanilla extract

2 small, fresh apples, peeled,
    cored and cut into rings

Maple syrup, for serving

1. Stir together the flours, sugar, baking powder, baking soda, salt, and cinnamon in a large mixing bowl.

2. In a food processor or blender, combine the almond milk, water, mashed sweet potato, melted coconut oil, flax seed, vinegar, and vanilla extract. Blend on high until smooth.

3. Add the wet ingredients to the dry ingredients, stirring until a rough batter forms; it shouldn't be totally smooth. Let the batter rest for 15 minutes.

4. When ready to cook, heat a nonstick frying pan or griddle over a medium heat. Grease with melted coconut oil.

5. Pour small ladles of batter into the pan, spaced apart, and place an apple ring on top of each. Let set and cook until golden brown underneath, 3 to 4 minutes, before flipping and cooking the other sides for another 3 minutes.

6. Slide out of the pan and keep warm, covered loosely with foil. Repeat for the remaining pancakes, greasing the pan with more coconut oil between batches.

7. Once all the pancakes are cooked, serve with a drizzle of maple syrup.

Baked Apple Cider Donuts

MAKES 12 DONUTS

Orchards are big business in the fall, and provide a unique brand of family entertainment. While there are plenty of no-frills orchards where serious pickers can go and harvest a winter's worth of fruit, many others have added hay rides, food, and live music. Orchards also provide a venue for neighboring farms to sell their produce. At most orchards, the scent of freshly fried cider doughnuts wafts through the chilly air in intermittent waves, advertising a seasonal treat almost impossible to resist. This baked version can be made at home with fresh cider from the orchard and without the trouble of deep frying.

Donuts

1½ cup fresh apple cider

Cooking spray

2 cups all-purpose flour

1 teaspoon baking soda

¾ teaspoon baking powder

1 teaspoon ground cinnamon

⅛ teaspoon ground cloves

⅛ teaspoon freshly grated nutmeg

¼ teaspoon salt

2 tablespoons unsalted butter, melted

1 large egg, at room temperature

½ cup light brown sugar, packed

½ cup granulated sugar

½ cup milk, at room temperature

1 teaspoon vanilla extract

Coating

1 cup granulated sugar

¾ teaspoon ground cinnamon

⅛ teaspoon ground cloves

¼ cup unsalted butter, melted

1. To make the donuts, reduce the apple cider in a saucepan set over a low heat until you have about ½ cup liquid left, 15 to 20 minutes depending on the pan. Remove the reduced cider from the heat and allow to cool completely.

2. Preheat the oven to 350°F. Spray a 12-cavity donut pan with cooking spray.

3. Whisk together the flour, baking soda, baking powder, spices, and salt in a large mixing bowl.

4. In a separate mixing bowl, thoroughly whisk together the reduced apple cider, melted butter, egg, sugars, milk, and vanilla.

5. Whisk the dry ingredients into the wet, mixing until you have a thick batter; it doesn't need to be totally smooth.

6. Divide the batter between the holes of the pan; you can use a piping bag for cleaner and easier filling.

7. Bake until set and browned at the edges, 10 to 12 minutes; they should feel a little springy to the touch when ready. Transfer the donuts to a cooling rack to cool.

8. To make the coating, pulse together the sugar and spices in a food processor. Tip out into a shallow dish.

9. Brush the donuts all over with melted butter and then coat in the sugar mix, turning to coat all over. Best served warm.

Baked Apples with Cider Sauce

SERVES 4

Use a sturdy apple for this dish, such as Honeycrisp, Paula Red, or Crispin, which won't fall apart while baking. It's important to note that the dry cider called for in the recipe refers to the bottled hard ciders produced by craft brewers; not the fresh cider you purchase from the orchard.

8 small- to medium-sized fresh apples, washed, cored, and cut in half horizontally

Juice of ½ lemon

1⅔ cups dry cider

½ cup brown sugar

1⅓ cups heavy cream

3 teaspoons maple syrup

Whiskey, to taste

1. Preheat the oven to 350°F.

2. Brush the cut surfaces of the apples with lemon juice and put the two halves back together.

3. Put the cider into a pan with the sugar and the rest of the lemon juice and boil until the sugar has dissolved. Put the apples into a baking dish, add the cider sauce, and bake in the preheated oven for about 1 hour.

4. Whip the cream with the maple syrup and whiskey until stiff peaks form.

5. When the apples are done, take them out of the oven, put a little cream into the middle of each, replace the top halves, and serve on plates with the cider sauce and the rest of the whipped cream.

SNELL FAMILY FARM

BUXTON

If you ever want to talk about plants, farming, food, and how it all makes you feel, Carolyn Snell—fourth-generation farmer—is all ears.

You'll find her slinging seedlings, vegetables, fruit, fresh flowers, and honest-to-goodness cheer at the Snell Family Farm stall at the Portland Farmers' Market, or at the farm's on-site store in Buxton.

Carolyn farms with her parents, John and Ramona, her sister-in-law Abby, and a crew of community members and neighbors on their land in Buxton, which has been operating as Snell Family Farm since her great-grandparents started growing apples and poultry in 1926. Through the middle of the century, Carolyn's grandfather, John Sr., focused primarily on apples. In the '70s, John Jr. and Ramona started growing vegetables to sell alongside the apples. The farm added greenhouse plants to the mix in 1986, which has been met with much enthusiasm. Cut flowers were always available at the the farm's market stand, but Carolyn has expanded the floral pro-

gram to include designs for weddings and special events. Raspberries and kitchen production are the most recent additions.

Today, the farm grows about 20 acres of vegetables, four acres of flowers, one acre of raspberries, and eight acres of apples.

"We grow food, flowers, and plants for our neighbors," Carolyn says of the farm's retail-based business model. "And we think of our relationship in the community as one of our crops."

The on-site farm store operates May 1 through Thanksgiving. The orchards open for pick-your-own fruit starting in mid-September and con-

tinue until the apples are gone. Trees also include peach, plum, pear, and tart cherries.

Carolyn went to college for writing and art and confesses she likes precise language. So it's no surprise that her favorite of the farm's passionate reviews over the years is brief and to the point:

"Very nice people, good prices. Not too fancy."

And to Carolyn, who believes it's her family farm's responsibility and mission to cultivate not only food and plants, but a culture of care for their fellow humans, this feels like the perfect Maine compliment.

Snell Farm Apple Pie

MAKES ONE 9-INCH PIE

Since 2015, Abby Snell—daughter-in-law to John and Ramona—has led the team at the farm kitchen. Says Abby, "It is such a joy to bake pies with apples fresh from the orchard, learning about new varieties and how different they look, taste, and smell." Abby uses a mix of early Lodi, Wealthy, and Cortland apples for the farm pies.

Crust

2 tablespoons water

2 tablespoons buttermilk

A couple of ice cubes

2½ cups all-purpose flour

1 tablespoon granulated sugar

1 teaspoon sea salt

2 sticks (8 ounces) unsalted butter, cut into small pieces and chilled

Filling

6 medium-sized fresh apples (Abby recommends a mix of both tart and sweet apples, but says most any apple will do)

1 tablespoon lemon juice

½ cup granulated sugar

¼ cup brown sugar

1 teaspoon cinnamon

¼ teaspoon nutmeg

3 tablespoons flour

Pinch of sea salt

1 teaspoon lemon zest

A little milk, for brushing on the crust (optional)

1. To make the crust, place the water and buttermilk into a measuring cup and add a couple of ice cubes to keep the liquid very cold.

2. Place the flour, sugar, and sea salt into the bowl of a stand mixer and mix on low speed for a couple seconds just to incorporate.

3. Sprinkle the chilled butter pieces evenly over the dry ingredients and mix on low until the butter is pea sized and the mixture looks a bit pebbly.

4. Add the cold water/buttermilk mixture and pulse on the lowest speed until the dough comes away from the sides of the bowl and holds together. If the dough is dry, add additional liquid 1 tablespoon at a time, mixing by hand until it just holds together.

5. Divide the dough in half, flatten into 2 disks, wrap tightly in plastic wrap, and chill at least one hour or overnight.

6. Roll out the dough disks on a well-floured surface, working in each direction until you have a nice round that is about ⅛-inch thick.

7. Use your rolling pin to gently roll up one of the rounds of dough like a scroll and then unroll it onto a 9-inch pie pan.

8. Settle the dough into the pie pan, and then cut a ½-inch margin around it with kitchen scissors.

9. Form the other rolled-out round of dough, cut a lid for the pie about the same diameter.

10. Chill these in the refrigerator until ready to fill. Preheat the oven to 425°F.

11. To make the filling, peel and slice the apples and toss them in a large bowl with some lemon juice to keep them from browning.

12. In a medium bowl, mix the sugars, cinnamon, nutmeg, flour, and sea salt with a whisk.

13. Mix the lemon zest with the apples, then add the dry ingredients and mix well. All the apple slices should be evenly coated with the dry mixture.

14. Arrange the filling in your prepared pie crust and place the dough lid on top.

15. Trim the edges of the dough if needed, and then crimp with a fork, your fingers, or some other decorative tool.

16. If desired, brush a little milk on top for a nicely browned and shiny crust. Slash the top crust to allow steam to escape.

17. Place the pie on a cookie sheet to catch any drippings and bake for 25 minutes. Rotate the pie and turn the oven down to 350°F.

18. Bake until the crust is golden brown and fruit juices are bubbling vigorously, about 35 to 40 minutes.

19. Allow to cool about 4 hours (if you can wait that long!).

OUT ON A LIMB APPLES CSA

PALERMO

What exactly is an apple CSA? In the case of Out on a Limb Apples, it's a program to promote and support Maine's apple heritage by making rare apples available to the general consumer.

The CSA is the brain child of apple historian and author John Bunker, who grows heirloom apples on his farm in Palermo. John is committed to tracking down and preserving Maine's forgotten and almost-lost apple varieties.

Many years ago, John compiled a list of orchards that had rare and heirloom apple varieties for apple lovers to visit. But when he realized that perhaps most people didn't possess as much apple-driven wanderlust as he did, he thought of a way to bring the apples to the people.

Out on a Limb Apples grows 100 varieties of mostly rare or historic apples, some of which they deliver to six pick-up locations from September to early November for their 150-member CSA. They also partner with other small, central Maine orchards that grow hard-to-find heirloom varieties to fill out each 12-pound delivery. In a single season, members will receive 20 or more varieties that they wouldn't otherwise find at the grocery store.

Out on a Limb Apples also does apple identification, as well as educational displays. The largest of these displays takes place every October as part of the annual Portland-based Heirloom Apple Tasting, organized in partnership with the popular blog, Portland Food Map.

Apple and Blackberry Crumble

SERVES 4

Make this crumble in the late summer, when the blackberries ripen just as the early apple varieties start appearing in local orchards. Early varieties in Maine include Lodi and the rare Gravenstein, which appear as early as mid-August.

Filling

1 pound fresh cooking apples, peeled, cored and chopped into chunks

11 ounces blackberries

¼ cup apple juice

4 tablespoons granulated sugar

Crumble

3½ ounces butter

½ cup brown sugar

½ cup all-purpose flour

½ cup chopped raw almonds

⅔ cup chopped raw hazelnuts

5 tablespoons rolled oats

1. Preheat the oven to 400°F.

2. To make the filling, stir together the apples, blackberries, apple juice, and sugar in a large bowl. Spill the coated fruit out into an 8-by-8-inch baking dish.

3. To make the crumble, place the butter, sugar, flour, and almonds in a food processor and pulse until the mixture resembles bread crumbs. Mix in the hazelnuts and oats.

4. Sprinkle the crumble over the filling and bake in the oven for 20 to 25 minutes, or until the fruit is bubbling and the crumble is toasted.

THE MAINE HERITAGE ORCHARD

UNITY

The ten-acre Maine Heritage Orchard is a preservation and educational orchard on the Maine Organic Farmers and Gardeners Association (MOFGA) grounds in Unity. Founded in 2014, the orchard is home to 300 varieties of apples and pears traditionally grown in Maine. Under the directorship of apple historian John Bunker, the orchard will eventually grow 500 varieties, preserving the historic, rare, and nearly extinct fruit of New England.

The project is largely powered by volunteers and runs several programs to encourage community participation. These include an annual tree-planting day on the orchard and a tree stewardship program for members of the Maine community that want to introduce these rare varieties on their own land.

Baked Pears with Blue Cheese and Slivered Almonds

SERVES 4

Maine pear varieties include Clapp's Favorite, Seckel, Bosc, Golden Spice, Beurre Giffard, and Bartlett, all of which are hardy and firm-fleshed. Nuts and strong, salty cheeses complement pears' delicate but distinctive flavors. For this recipe, use a soft, ripe blue cheese with a good balance of creamy and salty.

4 ripe firm pears, rinsed, halved vertically, and cored

2 tablespoons freshly squeezed lemon juice

4 ounces blue cheese

¼ cup sliced raw almonds

1. Preheat the oven to 350° F. Line a baking sheet with parchment paper.

2. Arrange the pears on the prepared baking sheet and brush the cut side of the pears with lemon juice. Bake for 10 to 15 minutes, or until slightly soft when pierced with a sharp knife.

3. Meanwhile, slice the blue cheese into 8 pieces. Remove the pears from oven and place a piece of cheese over the cut half of each pear and sprinkle sliced almonds over the cheese.

4. Return the pears to the oven and bake for an additional 5 minutes or until the cheese is melted and the almonds are golden brown.

5. Remove the pan from the oven and transfer pears to serving plates. Serve warm.

LOCUST GROVE

ALBION

Gordon Kenyon started planting peach trees more than 35 years ago and hasn't stopped. Currently, his hilltop orchard in central Maine grows 14 varieties of peaches from more than 1,000 trees.

Although not organic, Gordon does not treat his peaches with insecticide (organic or chemical), giving them an edge with health-focused consumers, since peaches are one of the most heavily sprayed crops on the market.

While not the largest peach orchard in Maine, Locust Grove is closely managed and not open to Pick Your Own sales. Gordon says this is his way of guaranteeing that peaches are picked from the tree only when perfectly ripe.

Now in his late 70s, Gordon is passing the orchard's reins to Colleen Hanlon-Smith, formerly the manager at Unity Food Hub.

Crème Anglaise with Grilled Nectarines or Peaches

SERVES 4

Maine-grown stone fruit such as peaches, nectarines, plums, and cherries are a unique brand all their own. Most grow small—especially compared to the behemoths of the Southern states and the orchards of California—but they are sweet and perfume-y, often with dark, compressed flesh that is satiny smooth. On the grill, these extra-sweet fruits caramelize beautifully, creating a buttery but firm base for the crème anglaise. And while nothing really equals the flavor imparted by cooking over fire, if you don't have a grill or can't grill due to weather, the show must go on! You can make use of your oven's broiler to impart a similar grilled flavor in your nectarines or peaches.

Crème Anglaise

1 cup heavy cream

¼ cup granulated sugar

1 teaspoon vanilla extract

3 large egg yolks, beaten

Fruit

4 ripe nectarines or peaches, rinsed, halved vertically, and pitted

2 tablespoons butter, melted

1 to 2 tablespoons granulated sugar

1. To make the crème anglaise, in a medium saucepan, combine the cream, sugar, and vanilla extract. Bring the mixture to a gentle boil over medium-low heat. Immediately remove pan from heat to stop the boiling.

2. Meanwhile, in a separate bowl, whisk the egg yolks to blend. Pouring in a slow stream, whisk in half of the warm cream to temper the eggs. Whisk the tempered egg mixture into the saucepan.

3. Return the cream-egg mixture to the saucepan and cook for about 5 minutes, stirring constantly. The mixture will thicken, but do not allow it to boil. Strain the custard into a bowl. Cover and refrigerate until completely chilled.

4. To make the nectarines or peaches, preheat the grill to medium. Brush the cut side of the fruit with the melted butter and sprinkle with sugar. Grill for 3 to 5 minutes on each side. Serve the fruit warm, drizzled with crème anglaise.

FROM THE BOG, BRAMBLE, AND BARREN

Blueberries, huckleberries, raspberries, strawberries, blackberries, service berries, elderberries, black and red currants—the small jewel-like fruits that grow in the farms, gardens, forests, and fields of Maine are diverse and colorful. Blueberries, a $48 million industry in the state, take first place in production among berries, and fourth in agricultural products in general, behind potatoes, dairy, and chicken eggs.

Wild blueberries are one of Maine's only truly native crops and are heralded for their superior flavor and health benefits. About 44,000 acres in Maine are dedicated to the stewardship and management of this wild crop, and 100 million pounds of blueberries are harvested during their relatively short season that starts in late July and ends in early September.

There are plenty of pick-your-own berry farms where pickers can don sunscreen and wide hats, collect pint- or quart-sized containers at the farm entrance, and make their way lazily down the rows of raspberry canes, or along rows lined with string on managed blueberry barrens. Farms will provide rakes for low bush wild blueberries, or pickers can bring their own. Many farms now also grow cultivated high-bush blueberries, which, for Pick Your Own purposes, are much easier as they don't require hours of crouching.

Elderberry Blinis with Caramelized Apples

SERVES 4

Elderberries, long known for their curative health benefits, are growing in popularity among modern herbalists and other natural health practitioners in Maine. They are a favorite among home canners for jelly and can be grown in home gardens and found occasionally at a roadside farm stand. If you are lucky enough to come upon a handful or two of this uniquely flavored fruit, this recipe is a quick and easy way to celebrate them.

Blinis

1 cup sifted whole wheat flour

1½ teaspoons baking powder

½ teaspoon sea salt

½ cup rolled oats

½ teaspoon baking soda

1 teaspoon ground cinnamon

1 large egg

1 cup buttermilk

2 tablespoons sunflower oil, or other cooking oil

1 tablespoon water

2 small eating apples, unpeeled and grated

¼ cup fresh elderberries (see Tip)

Caramelized Apples

¼ cup butter

4 eating apples, peeled and diced

4 tablespoons granulated sugar

2 teaspoons ground cinnamon

For Serving

Confectioners' sugar

Honey

Yogurt

1. To make the blinis, combine the flour, baking powder, sea salt, oats, baking soda, and cinnamon in a mixing bowl.

2. In a separate bowl, whisk together the egg, buttermilk, 1 tablespoon of the oil, and the water. Stir in the grated apples and elderberries.

3. Stir the buttermilk mixture into the dry ingredients to make a thick batter.

4. Heat a little oil in a cast-iron skillet or heavy frying pan.

5. Spoon about 2 tablespoons of the batter into the hot pan. Cook for 3 to 4 minutes until bubbles start to appear on the surface of each blini. Flip, and gently cook on the other side for another 3 to 4 minutes, until the blinis are cooked through.

6. Repeat until all the batter is used, layering the blinis between parchment on a plate.

7. To make the caramelized apples, heat the butter in a frying pan and add the apples, sugar, and cinnamon. Cook over medium heat for about 10 minutes, turning occasionally until evenly caramelized.

8. Layer the blinis with the caramelized apples. Sift confectioners' sugar over the top of each stack, and drizzle with honey. Serve with yogurt.

Tip: Do not eat raw elderberries. They must be cooked to be edible.

NORIMOTO BAKERY

SOUTH PORTLAND

When Portland's beloved French-Japanese fusion patisserie Ten Ten Pié closed unexpectedly in 2019, baker Atsuko Fujimoto didn't wait for another job offer. The seasoned baker, who earned her pastry chops in the kitchens of Fore Street Restaurant and Standard Baking Co., took to the streets of Portland to provide her signature danishes, savory pies, and desserts for coffee shops and restaurants under the new moniker Norimoto Bakery. While renting kitchen space from her fellow bakers at Two Fat Cats, Atsuko is working to grow back her wholesale business, and also provide direct-to-customer sales a few days per week from the Two Fat Cats South Portland location. The energetic baker manages all her own deliveries each morning between baking shifts.

Atsuko, a former magazine editor, moved to Maine from Tokyo in 2001 and was immediately inspired by the high-quality produce and seafood available. "I'm not sure I would have become a baker if I hadn't moved to Maine," Atsuko says.

Her pastries, featuring fruits and vegetables from her own gardens, are an accurate reflec-

tion of the growing seasons in Maine. Rhubarb and strawberry danishes in the spring; blueberry, raspberry, blackberry, peach, and plum hand pies in the summer; sour cherry, apple, pear, and quince galettes in the fall. Many of her creations carry influences of her former home—sake cakes, green tea custard danish, traditional babkas spiked with sweet adzuki bean paste.

"In general, I like food that clearly tells you what you are eating," Atsuko says. "If I make rhubarb Danish, I want people to really taste the intense tartness of rhubarb."

Norimoto's danishes—buttery delicacies layered with flaky laminated croissant dough, creamy custardy filling, and fresh seasonal fruits—are locally famous and are in part what inspired *Bon Appétit* to declare Portland the magazine's Restaurant City of the Year in 2018.

While Atsuko appreciates the freedom of leasing kitchen space for her wholesale business, she hopes to eventually find a permanent home for Norimoto, possibly with counter and coffee service and room for her faithful clientele to sit and enjoy her pastries.

Cranberry-Orange Scones with Citrus Glaze

MAKES 15 SCONES

Cranberries grow in both dry and wet bogs in Maine, often surrounded by stands of cedar and soft fluffy carpets of peat moss. Cranberries ripen in mid to late fall, and appear on market shelves all over the state in time for Thanksgiving and the Christmas holidays. But ripe berries can also winter over and be picked during a second (much smaller) harvest in the early spring when things thaw out. Fresh cranberries freeze extremely well, with no special preparation.

This recipe utilizes dried cranberries, which are often sold alongside other dried fruits such as raisins and apricots. However, for an extra-tart, uniquely textured scone, substitute ½ to ¾ cup fresh cranberries for the dried.

Scones

4¼ cups all-purpose flour

¼ cup granulated sugar, plus extra for sprinkling

2 teaspoons orange zest

2 teaspoons salt

2 tablespoons baking powder

1½ cups (12 ounces) unsalted butter, cold and cubed

4 fresh extra-large eggs, lightly beaten

1 cup heavy cream, chilled

1 cup dried cranberries

1 fresh egg

2 tablespoons water

Citrus Glaze

½ cup confectioners' sugar, sifted

1 tablespoon fresh squeezed orange juice

1. Preheat the oven to 400° F. Line a baking sheet with parchment paper.

2. In the bowl of an electric mixer, using the paddle attachment, mix 4 cups flour, the granulated sugar, orange zest, salt, and baking powder together. Reduce mixer speed to low. Add the cold butter and mix until the butter is crumbly.

3. In a separate bowl, combine the eggs and heavy cream. With the mixer on low speed, gradually add the egg mixture to the flour and butter mixture, mixing until just blended. Toss the cranberries in the remaining ¼ cup flour and add to the dough mixture. Mix at low speed until blended.

4. Place the dough on a well-floured work surface or board and knead it into a ball. Flour your rolling pin and your hands and roll out the dough to a thickness of just under 1 inch. You will see small bits of butter in the dough. Flour a 3-inch round cutter and cut out circles of dough. Place the cut dough on the prepared baking sheet. Use the scraps to roll out and cut more circles.

5. Mix the egg and water to make the egg wash, then brush the tops of the scones. Sprinkle with granulated sugar and bake for 20 to 25 minutes, or until the tops are golden brown. The scones should be firm to the touch. Cool on wire racks for 15 minutes.

6. Whisk together confectioners' sugar and orange juice. Place wire rack with scones over the baking sheet; drizzle glaze over scones. Serve.

RED BOG ORGANIC CRANBERRIES

SEDGWICK

Sisters Dale and Kipp Quinby didn't set out to become cranberry farmers when they bought land on the Blue Hill Peninsula a few years ago. The sisters grew up working on the water with their dad, a marine specimen harvester based first on Isle au Haut, then Sedgwick. Dale worked at the local library, Kipp was a commercial fisherman, and neither had ever managed a cranberry bog.

But when the previous harvester who leased the two bogs on their property decided to retire, the Quinbys—always open to learning new things—grabbed a couple of rakes and went into the cranberry business.

Certified organic by MOFGA, Red Bog cran-berries are not treated with fungicides or other chemicals; rather, the insects and fungus are managed by flooding the bogs each spring. Ulti-mately, this produces a small harvest, but Dale and Kipp feel strongly about agricultural prac-tices that benefit the land, the animal and insect communities that live there, and the health of their customers.

The sisters harvest their bogs with a combina-tion of hand and mechanical raking, hand-pack their retail cartons, and sell them locally at the Blue Hill Co-op, the local grocery market, and through a distributor that delivers them to food co-ops and farmers' markets throughout Maine.

Sweet Potato Blueberry Muffins

MAKES 2 DOZEN MUFFINS

Whole wheat flour gives these blueberry muffins a pleasant grain flavor. Use a freshly milled one, if possible. Sweet potatoes add sublime texture and moisture and ensure that your muffins will never be dry. If you are using frozen blueberries, there is no need to thaw them; in fact, it's better if you don't. Adding the berries frozen will benefit the dough by instantly chilling it and will prevent turning all of it instantly blue.

1½ cups cooked mashed sweet potatoes,
    cooled (or use canned sweet potatoes)

1 cup light brown sugar, packed

3 large eggs

5 tablespoons orange juice

5 tablespoons canola or sunflower oil

2 cups sifted whole wheat flour

1 cup all-purpose flour

2½ teaspoons baking powder

1½ teaspoons cinnamon, ground

¾ teaspoon salt

¼ teaspoon baking soda

2 cups blueberries, fresh or frozen

1. Preheat the oven to 350°F.

2. In a large bowl, stir together the sweet potatoes, brown sugar, eggs, orange juice, and oil until smooth.

3. In a separate bowl, stir together the flours, baking powder, cinnamon, salt, and baking soda.

4. Add the dry ingredients to the sweet potato mixture and stir until combined.

5. Stir in the blueberries. Divide into 24 paper-lined muffin cups. Bake for 30 to 35 minutes, until lightly browned.

Blackberry and Almond Torte

SERVES 8

I prefer using wild dead-ripe blackberries for this torte rather than the large cultivated ones found in the grocery stores. Small, wild blackberries tend to be sweeter and softer, and stud this unusual cake—redolent with the scent of almonds and vanilla—with attractive bright purple stains.

1¼ cups (9 ounces) unsalted butter,
    softened, plus extra for greasing

1¼ cups granulated sugar

1 cup (about 9 ounces by weight) almond
    paste, at room temperature

1½ teaspoons vanilla extract

6 large eggs, at room temperature

1 cup all-purpose flour

2 tablespoons cornstarch

2 tablespoons ground almonds

1½ teaspoons baking powder

¼ teaspoon salt

2 tablespoons milk

1½ cups blackberries

Confectioners' sugar, for serving

1. Preheat the oven to 350°F.

2. Line the bottom of an 8-inch springform pan with parchment paper. Grease the paper and up the sides of the pan with soft butter and dust with a little flour, tipping out the excess.

3. Pulse together the sugar and almond paste in a food processor until crumbly in appearance.

4. Add the butter and vanilla extract, processing until the mixture is smooth.

5. Blend the eggs into the mixture, one at a time, processing thoroughly between additions.

6. Spoon and scrape the mixture into a large mixing bowl. Sprinkle over the sifted flour, cornstarch, ground almonds, baking powder, and salt, cutting and folding until a smooth batter forms. Stir in the milk.

7. Transfer the batter to the prepared tin. Dust the blackberries with a little flour before pressing into the batter.

8. Bake for 40 to 55 minutes until golden, risen, and slightly springy to the touch; a toothpick should come out clean from the center.

9. Remove the cake to a wire rack and cool completely before turning out, slicing, and serving with a light dusting of confectioners' sugar.

TWO FAT CATS BAKERY

PORTLAND AND SOUTH PORTLAND

If baker Stacy Begin ever has time between work and family to take a break, you might find her in a comfy chair on her front porch enjoying a treat from her own bakery. "It is never a bad day when you have the chance to slow down, sit in the sun, and eat pie," she says.

It was with that precept that Stacy and her husband Matthew Holbrook purchased Portland-based Two Fat Cats Bakery in 2012, taking over the well-laureled legacy of locally famous restaurateur Dana Street (Fore Street Restaurant, Street & Co.) and James Beard award–winning baker Alison Pray (Standard Baking Co.).

The bakery specializes in rustic, American-style, made-from-scratch baked goods. While they are known nationally for their pies, they also make celebration cakes, cookies, bars, and whoopie pies.

With Stacy at the helm, the bakery has more than doubled sales while adapting to new commerce platforms and the changing palates of modern pastry lovers. "From vegan pies to buckwheat chocolate chip cookies, we've experimented more with different baking ingredients and techniques to meet the customers' evolving tastes," says Stacy.

The bakery uses local eggs and dairy for their baked goods, as well as strawberries, apples, peaches, rhubarb, and native wild blueberries. Their blueberry pie is featured on restaurant menus throughout the area and is their best-selling product nationally through the curated foodie website, Goldbelly.

Stacy attributes the bakery's success to a loyal, creative staff. "I am . . . proud of the collaborative, engaging culture we have created at the bakery," she says. "Our team is truly extraordinary at what they do; but more importantly, they are kind, warm, generous people. It is a privilege to work with them."

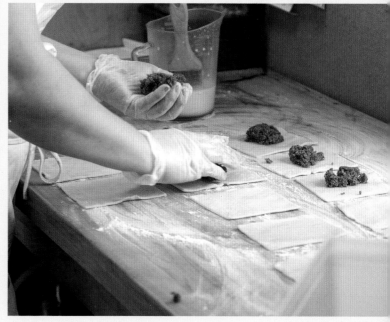

Two Fat Cats Lemon Zucchini Whoopie Pies with Blueberry Filling

MAKES 12 FOUR-INCH WHOOPIE PIES, OR 24 MINIS

In 2011, the state legislature decreed the whoopie pie the official Maine state treat. A traditional whoopie pie is made with a sweet white frosting-like filling sandwiched between two small chocolate cakes. For those who want a break from tradition, bakeries usually offer some non-traditional whoopie pie varieties. This summery version, adapted from the Two Fat Cats bakery recipe, requires some work, but the final result will make you the star of the next potluck.

Cakes

4 cups all-purpose flour

2 teaspoons baking soda

2 teaspoons baking powder

1 teaspoon sea salt

8 tablespoons unsalted butter, at room temperature

1 cup granulated sugar

1 cup brown sugar

6 tablespoons oil

2 large eggs

¾ cup whole milk

6 ounces shredded zucchini

4 teaspoons grated lemon zest

Filling

12 ounces fresh Maine blueberries

½ cup granulated sugar

2 tablespoons cornstarch

2 teaspoons lemon juice

Meringue

4 large egg whites

¼ teaspoon cream of tartar

A pinch of sea salt

1⅓ cups granulated sugar

⅓ cup water

1 pound unsalted butter

2 teaspoons vanilla extract

Confectioners' sugar (optional)

1. To make the cakes, preheat the oven to 350°F. Grease two baking sheets, or line them with parchment.

2. In a large bowl, whisk together the flour, baking soda, baking powder, and sea salt.

3. In the bowl of a stand mixer, beat together the butter, granulated sugar, brown sugar, and oil. Beat in the eggs.

4. Add the dry ingredients and the milk alternately to the butter mixture in three additions, beginning and ending with the dry ingredients. Beat well.

5. Stir in the shredded zucchini and lemon zest.

6. Using a 2-ounce scoop, place six mounds of batter on each cookie sheet, leaving 2 inches between mounds. This will use half the batter.

7. Bake the cakes for 15 to 20 minutes, rotating the pans once. The cakes are done when they are dry and spring back when you press them lightly with your finger.

8. Remove them from the oven, transfer to a cooling rack, and then repeat steps 6 and 7 with the remaining batter.

9. To make the filling, place the blueberries, sugar, cornstarch, and lemon juice in a medium-sized saucepan. Cook over medium heat until the sugar dissolves and the mixture bubbles. Stir constantly until thickened, resembling the texture of jam. Remove from the heat and set aside.

10. Place the egg whites in the clean, grease-free bowl of your stand mixer. Add the cream of tartar and beat with a whisk attachment on high until the whites hold soft peaks. Slowly add ⅓ cup of the granulated sugar and beat until the whites are fairly stiff, but not dry.

11. Meanwhile, place the remaining 1 cup sugar and water in a small saucepan, and bring to a boil over medium-high heat. Cook the syrup until the temperature registers 242°F on an instant thermometer. The syrup will be glossy and slightly viscous, with bubbles forming and popping.

12. Immediately remove the sugar from the heat and pour about ¼ cup of it into the meringue. Turn the mixer on to high and continue to pour the syrup into the meringue in a slow steady stream, taking care not to hit the whisk attachment.

13. When all the syrup is incorporated, continue to beat the meringue on high until it is cool to the touch.

14. With the mixer going, add the soft butter in large spoonfuls, beating until smooth after each addition. When all the butter is added, continue to beat until the buttercream is silky smooth. Beat in the vanilla extract. If at any time the buttercream gets soupy or separates, just keep beating. It will eventually come together and your stand mixer will have earned its keep.

15. Stir the cooled blueberry compote into the buttercream. You don't have to add all of it, and you don't need to mix it thoroughly—a few dark streaks makes a pretty filling.

16. Place about 3 to 4 ounces of filling on the flat surface of one cake. Top with another cake, rounded side up. Press down on the top cake so that the filling spreads to the edges. Repeat with the rest of the cakes.

17. Serve on a platter, and dust the whoopie pies with confectioners' sugar, if desired.

Blueberry Buckle

SERVES 8

Crunchy-topped with a soft interior streaked generously with blueberries, this cake is just as good for breakfast as it is for dessert. For the best slicing, leave plenty of time for the cake to cool completely before serving. Tossing fresh blueberries with flour before stirring them into the batter will help prevent them from turning everything blue. Alternatively, you can use frozen blueberries.

¼ cup soft unsalted butter, plus extra for greasing

2 cups all-purpose flour, plus 2 tablespoons extra for dusting blueberries

2 teaspoons baking powder

½ teaspoon salt

¾ cup granulated sugar

1 large egg

½ cup whole milk

3 cups fresh blueberries

Topping

¼ cup unsalted butter

½ cup granulated sugar

⅓ cup all-purpose flour

½ teaspoon ground cinnamon

1. Preheat the oven to 350°F. Grease an 8-inch square cake pan with butter.

2. Whisk together 2 cups flour, baking powder, and salt in a mixing bowl.

3. In a stand mixer, beat together the butter and granulated sugar on a moderate speed until pale and creamy, 2 to 3 minutes. Add the egg, beating well to incorporate.

4. On a lower speed, beat in flour mixture and milk in three parts, beginning and ending with the flour, until batter is smooth.

5. Toss the blueberries with 2 tablespoons flour and gently fold into batter. Spoon batter into prepared pan and rap a few times on a flat surface to help it settle.

6. To make the topping, rub together the remaining butter, granulated sugar, flour, and the cinnamon in a mixing bowl until crumbly. Spoon the topping over the batter in an even layer.

7. Bake the cake for 50 to 60 minutes until risen and golden brown on top; a wooden toothpick should come out clean from the center.

8. Remove the pan to a wire rack, and let the cake cool in the pan. When ready to serve, turn it out and cut into slices.

BETH'S FARM MARKET

WARREN

In 1979, Beth Ahlholm and her husband Vince bought White Oak Farm—then consisting of just a few acres—from Vince's father. Their first "market" was a stand on the side of road where they sold corn.

Since then, the Ahlholms have grown the farm to over 300 acres of diversified fruit and vegetable production—mostly on unconnected patches of land throughout Knox County.

And their farm stand—known simply as Beth's—has become one of the most visited and celebrated in Maine. They sell over 100 different kinds of fruits and vegetables, and declare from their iconic chalkboard inside the stand, "Everything sold here is grown here"—including farm stand regulars like corn, beans, and cucumbers. But Beth's also offers crops introduced to them by their Jamaican co-workers—okra and callaloo.

When the farm's strawberry season starts you can expect to see their small but sweet berries in stores up and down the Maine coast into October, their ever-bearing variety boasting a 120-day season. And the stand is famous for its house-made, James Beard Foundation–acclaimed strawberry shortcake, made with unsweetened berries and locally produced cream.

The stand is open from mid-April through Christmas, segueing into wreath and tree sales after harvest season winds down in November.

Strawberry Shortcake

SERVES 4

Some things are best eaten at their place of origin, and the Beth's Farm Stand strawberry shortcake is one of those things. There's just no recreating the dense cream, naturally super sweet berries, and fluffy biscuits. That said, this recipe is simple, good with both tart and sweet berries, and endlessly adaptable to other berries and fruits.

1 pound fresh strawberries

Up to 5 tablespoons granulated sugar

½ teaspoon vanilla extract

1 cup heavy cream, cold

4 Buttermilk Biscuits (page 34)

Fresh mint, for serving (optional)

1. Stem, hull, and slice the strawberries. Place them in a bowl and stir in 2 to 4 tablespoons of the sugar, depending on the berries' natural sweetness. Stir in the vanilla extract. Allow the berries to macerate at room temperature for at least ½ hour.

2. Place the cream in a chilled metal bowl and add 1 tablespoon of sugar. Whip the cream until it forms soft peaks.

3. To serve, split each biscuit in two horizontally. Place the bottom half in a bowl and spoon about ⅛ of the strawberries and their syrup over it. Scoop on some whipped cream, top with the other biscuit half, add another ⅛ of the strawberry-syrup mixture. Top with another dollop of whipped cream, and garnish with a sprig of mint if desired. Repeat with the other biscuits, using up all the strawberries and whipped cream.

Raspberry Tiramisu

SERVES 4

If you don't have a way of brewing espresso in your kitchen, you can purchase a good-quality instant espresso—such as Medaglia d'Oro—at most grocery stores. For a boozy kick, you can also substitute part or all of the espresso with coffee liqueur such as Kahlúa, or even Allen's Coffee Brandy, a favorite among salty Mainers. Fresh, tiny, ripe raspberries are pressed into the mascarpone here, and the entire dessert benefits from a long rest in the refrigerator. This not only gives the ladyfingers time to absorb all the flavors, but the raspberries will release their juices and perfume the entire confection with their essence.

30 sponge ladyfingers

1⅓ cups brewed, cold espresso

Grated zest and juice of 1 large lemon

2¼ cups mascarpone

3 tablespoons granulated sugar

3 cups fresh raspberries, rinsed and dried

⅔ cup grated bittersweet chocolate

1 tablespoon unsweetened cocoa powder

1. Line the base of an 8-inch square baking dish with half of the sponge ladyfingers. Brush each ladyfinger with the espresso coffee (using about half of the espresso).

2. In a medium bowl, combine lemon zest and juice, mascarpone, and sugar, mixing well to incorporate. Carefully spread ⅓ of the mascarpone over the ladyfingers in the baking dish. Scatter half of the raspberries over the mascarpone and gently press in, spread half of the remaining mascarpone over the raspberries. Sprinkle a generous amount of grated chocolate over the top. Arrange another layer of ladyfingers on top of the mascarpone and brush with the remaining espresso. Spread the remaining mascarpone on top.

3. Dust the entire surface generously with cocoa powder. Arrange the remaining raspberries on top and sprinkle with the remaining grated chocolate. Chill for at least 3 hours before serving.

Blueberry Ginger Cake

SERVES 12

My career in chocolate-making has required me to think well outside the box when it comes to pairing chocolate with unique ingredients. One of my favorite desserts is a dense chocolate gingerbread, spiked with molasses and treacle, generous amounts of dried, powdered ginger, and a spicy splash of strong ginger ale. This dessert boasts a similar unusual pairing of molasses and blueberries, deepening the celebratory summer fruit into something brooding and misty—like an abandoned blueberry barren in the fall. Make this in the shoulder month between summer and fall—when you're craving baked goods made with warm spices and there are still fresh blueberries in the stores.

½ cup (4 ounces) unsalted butter

1 cup granulated sugar

1 large egg

2 cups unbleached all-purpose flour

½ teaspoon ground ginger

1 teaspoon cinnamon

½ teaspoon salt

1 teaspoon baking soda

1 cup buttermilk

3 tablespoons molasses

1 cup fresh Maine blueberries

3 tablespoons cinnamon sugar, for sprinkling

1. Preheat the oven to 350° F. Grease and flour a 9-inch square cake pan.

2. In a large mixing bowl, cream the butter and sugar together. Add the egg and mix well.

3. Sift flour, ginger, cinnamon, and salt together. Dissolve the baking soda in the buttermilk. Add the dry mixture and buttermilk to the creamed mixture, alternating between the dry mixture and the buttermilk. Mix well.

4. Add the molasses, mixing to incorporate. Gently fold in the blueberries.

5. Pour batter immediately into the prepared pan. Sprinkle the cinnamon sugar on top of the batter. Bake for 50 to 60 minutes, or until a cake tester inserted into the center of the cake comes out clean. Cool in the pan on a wire rack for 5 to 10 minutes before serving.

Raspberry Trifle

SERVES 4

The ginger cookies and fresh raspberries make all
the difference in this simple trifle. Northern Maine
has a large Swedish population and so finding the
snappy, thin ginger cookies that Swedes can't live
without is as simple as going to the local grocery
store.

1½ cups heavy cream

**8 ounces chocolate ice cream, removed
from the freezer for 20 minutes**

**5 ounces ginger cookies (such as Swedish
ginger thins), crumbled**

2 cups fresh raspberries

1. Whip the cream until stiff peaks form.

2. Spread half of the softened ice cream into a large
glass bowl or trifle dish and smooth the top. Scatter
the ice cream with half of the ginger cookies and
press down slightly.

3. Spread half the whipped cream over the ice
cream–cookie layer and scatter over half the
raspberries.

4. Repeat step 2 and finish with a layer of whipped
cream. Scatter the remaining raspberries on top, put
the bowl into the freezer for about 10 minutes, and
serve immediately.

Blueberry Tart

SERVES 8

The amount of cornstarch you choose to use in the blueberry filling depends on how firm you like your tart. For example, if I'm serving this tart on a plate for dessert, then I will use the lesser amount of cornstarch. If I am bringing the tart to a picnic, I will use the larger amount so that the slices are clean, drip-free, and can be eaten out of hand. This is the best, easiest, most rewarding dessert I know how to make, and if you've unburied it from the pages of this cookbook, then you have found a true treasure.

Crust

¼ cup granulated sugar

1 teaspoon vanilla extract

½ teaspoon sea salt

8 tablespoons butter, melted

1 cup all-purpose flour

Filling

5 cups fresh blueberries

1 cup granulated sugar

2 to 4 tablespoons cornstarch

Topping

⅓ cup all-purpose flour

⅓ cup rolled oats

⅓ cup dark brown sugar

¼ teaspoon ground cardamom

½ teaspoon ground cinnamon

4 tablespoons butter, melted

1. Preheat the oven to 375°F.

2. To make the crust, put the sugar, vanilla, and salt in small bowl. Stir in the melted butter. Add the flour and stir until a very loose dough forms. Press the crust all over the bottom and up the sides of a 9-inch tart pan with a removable bottom.

3. To make the filling, place the blueberries and the sugar in a large bowl. Sift in the cornstarch. Mix the ingredients with your hands, mashing handfuls of blueberries as you go so the liquid binds up the dry ingredients a bit and allows everything to mix evenly. Scrape the filling into the tart pan. It's a lot of filling, so mound it up in the middle if you need to.

4. To make the topping, mix all the ingredients together in a bowl, then scatter them on top of the tart. Press it down with your hands to help it stay put.

5. Bake the tart until the filling is bubbling and the crust is golden. Cool completely before serving.

BLUE HILL BERRY CO.

PENOBSCOT

When Nicolas Lindholm and his wife, Ruth Fiske, purchased their Penobscot farmland in 1996 to grow cultivated vegetables to sell at local farmers' markets, they never imagined their life would eventually center around blueberries—a wild crop native to Maine.

The couple originally named their venture Hackmatack Farm, after the deciduous pine that grows in the coastal Maine forests, and focused on growing market vegetables for locals and area restaurants. But when Nicolas started exhibiting symptoms of Lyme disease and suffering from acute autoimmune issues related to the illness, all that changed.

"I couldn't keep the hours necessary for growing those kinds of crops and so we made the decision to stop market vegetable production in 2015, and focus exclusively on blueberry production," Nicolas explains.

Their land just happened to have 10 acres of blueberry fields on it, and so Nicolas started learning the stewardship of Maine's most famous wild crop.

"'Wild' is a bit of a misnomer," Nicolas explains. "The wild, or low-bush, blueberry is actually very intensively managed. A more accurate term would be 'native', as this is the place on Earth where they originate."

Nicolas was inspired by the health benefits of blueberries, particularly for helping his own symptoms stemming from Lyme disease, and discovered that wild Maine blueberries have more antioxidants than any other type of cultivated blueberry. He learned to manage his fields organically, encouraging a broad biodiversity in the field, both above and below the soil, to maintain healthy plants and control pests, disease, and weeds.

Now, Nicolas and his family manage 10 fields in five towns across the Blue Hill Peninsula, totaling 70 acres that produce about 30,000 pounds of blueberries annually. The Blue Hill Berry Co. is also one of only two blueberry producers in Maine that ship frozen blueberries directly from the farm.

WILD FERN PIES

SEDGWICK

Sarah Havener Brown began selling her pies and baked goods, made in her home kitchen from things that grew in her local farms and gardens, in 2011. Doing business as Sarahndipity Pies at the time, she sold her pastries—which grew to a menu of various baked goods and breakfast sandwiches—at farmers' markets and local shops, eventually going mobile in a colorful community-funded food wagon. At her busiest, she also managed a side hustle of wedding cakes with no help beyond her husband, Ellery, who occasionally serves as a pinch-hitting dishwasher.

These days, Sarah bakes with three small children at her feet, producing pies alone for the

markets at nearby Four Season and Roaring Lion Farms, and for special order. After the birth of her third child, she retired the food wagon and renamed her homestead bakery for her tousle-haired daughter, Matilda Fern.

Sarah's pies reflect the local wild and agricultural landscape that make up her immediate surroundings—fillings made from native low-bush blueberries, foraged apples, spring rhubarb, June strawberries, and cranberries from a nearby bog.

Wild Fern Apple-Cranberry Pie

MAKES ONE 9-INCH PIE

Sarah Havener Brown, owner of Wild Fern Pies, says she enjoys a slice of pie best in a rare solitary moment, sitting in a favorite chair, and looking out the window. A Maine native, Sarah's love for her home state is echoed in her baked goods, particularly this fall-inspired pie bursting with fresh, foraged apples and just-ripened cranberries.

Double Crust

2 cups all-purpose flour

2 teaspoons granulated sugar

1 teaspoon salt

8 ounces (2 sticks) unsalted butter, cold, cut into small cubes

5 to 7 tablespoons cold water

Filling

6 large, fresh apples—several different varieties if possible

4 tablespoons (¼ stick) unsalted butter

1 tablespoon maple syrup

1½ cups fresh or frozen cranberries

1 tablespoon apple pie spice

1 teaspoon ground ginger

½ cup granulated sugar

⅛ teaspoon salt

2 tablespoons cornstarch

1. To make the double crust, mix the flour, sugar, and salt together in a stand mixer with a paddle attachment.

2. Add the cubes of cold butter and mix on medium-low speed until the mixture resembles cornmeal.

3. Slowly add the cold water until a shaggy dough forms. Do not over-mix.

4. Split the dough in half, press each half into a disk, and wrap the disks in plastic. Place them in the refrigerator to rest for at least 30 minutes.

5. To make the filling, preheat the oven to 400°. Peel and slice apples to about ¼-inch thickness.

6. Melt the butter in a large cast-iron pan over medium heat. Add the sliced apples and the maple syrup and sauté for about 2 minutes.

7. Add cranberries, spices, sugar, salt, and cornstarch to the sautéed apples and give everything a good stir. Transfer the filling to a heat-proof bowl to cool.

8. Roll out one-half of the chilled pie dough to fit a 9-inch pie pan with about 1 inch in overhang.

9. Pour in the cooled filling and level.

10. Roll out the other disk of pie dough and lay it over the filling. Trim, crimp, and tuck the top and bottom crusts. Slash the top crust through in any design you like.

11. Bake the pie for 10 minutes, then reduce the heat to 350°F and bake for another 40 minutes, or until the top crust is golden and the filling is bubbling.

12. Let the pie cool before slicing and serving.

Rhubarb Tart with Strawberries, Mascarpone, and Rhubarb Coulis

SERVES 8

Rhubarb, a harbinger of Maine spring, fosters passionate feelings on both sides of the love it-hate it fence. But everyone usually agrees that its appearance in yards and fields across Maine in May is a welcome sight, as it means winter is, at long last, over. Rhubarb is a traditional and tasty partner to early summer strawberries, and this recipe is a somewhat fancier alternative to rustic strawberry-rhubarb pies and crumbles. It is worthy for a formal spring dinner party, striking, and utterly delicious.

Crust

2 cups all-purpose flour, plus extra for dusting

⅓ cup granulated sugar

¼ teaspoon salt

⅔ cup unsalted butter, cold and cubed

1 large egg yolk

1 teaspoon vanilla extract

Poached Rhubarb

1 liter water

1 cup granulated sugar

1 cinnamon stick

6 large (1½ pounds) rhubarb stalks, trimmed and cut in half

Filling

½ cup (4 ounces) unsalted butter, softened

½ cup granulated sugar

1 cup almond flour

3 large eggs, at room temperature

1 tablespoon cornstarch

1 teaspoon vanilla extract

For Serving

2 large (about ½ pound) rhubarb stalks, trimmed and diced

⅓ cup granulated sugar

1 teaspoon finely grated lemon zest

3 cups hulled and sliced strawberries

¼ cup water

1 vanilla bean

1 cup mascarpone

⅓ cup confectioners' sugar, sifted

2 tablespoons roughly chopped candied nuts, such as walnuts or pistachios

1 handful borage flowers (optional)

1. To make the crust, pulse together the flour, sugar, and salt in a food processor until combined. Add the butter and pulse until the mixture resembles fine bread crumbs.

2. Add the egg yolk and vanilla extract, pulsing until a rough dough forms around the blades. If needed, add a splash of cold water to help bring it together.

3. Turn out the dough and pat it down into a disk. Wrap it in plastic wrap and chill for 1 hour.

4. To make the poached rhubarb, combine the water, sugar, and cinnamon stick in a heavy-bottomed saucepan. Bring to a rapid simmer, stirring until sugar has dissolved.

5. Add the rhubarb to the saucepan, cover with a lid, and simmer over a low heat until tender to the tip of a knife, 12 to 15 minutes.

11. To make the filling, in a stand mixer, beat together the butter and sugar on a moderate speed until pale and creamy, about 3 minutes.

12. On a low speed, alternately beat in almond flour and eggs, one by one, until just combined. Beat in the cornstarch and vanilla extract.

13. Spoon the filling into the baked crust, spreading out evenly with the back of a damp tablespoon or an offset spatula.

14. Remove the cooled, poached rhubarb from the syrup and drain on paper towels. Arrange on top of the filling, side-by-side in rows—you may need to trim the ends to fit them.

15. Bake the tart for 40 to 50 minutes, or until filling is golden brown and slightly puffed. Remove to a cooling rack.

16. To serve: As the tart cools, combine the diced rhubarb, sugar, and lemon zest with half the strawberries and the water in a heavy-bottomed saucepan.

17. Bring to a boil, cover, and cook over low heat until the fruit is very tender, 10 to 12 minutes.

18. Using a slotted spoon, transfer the fruit to a food processor or blender and purée until smooth; if needed, thin out with some poaching liquid.

19. Pass the puree through a fine sieve into a serving bowl. Let cool to room temperature.

20. Split the vanilla bean lengthwise and scrape out the seeds into a mixing bowl. Add the mascarpone, confectioners' sugar, and a splash of warm water, beating until smooth. Cover and chill until ready to serve.

21. When ready to serve, turn out the tart from pan onto a serving platter. Decorate with remaining strawberries, chopped nuts, and borage flowers, if desired. Serve with the mascarpone and rhubarb coulis on side.

6. Remove the saucepan from the heat and let the rhubarb cool in the syrup.

7. After the dough has chilled, let it rest at room temperature for 10 minutes. Preheat the oven to 375°F.

8. Roll out the dough on a lightly floured surface into a large rectangle about ¼-inch thick. Use it to line the base and sides of a 14-by-5¾-by-1-inch fluted tart pan with a removable bottom.

9. Trim away any excess overhanging dough and prick the base all over with a fork. Line the dough with a sheet of parchment paper and fill with baking beans or rice. Place the pan on a rimmed baking sheet.

10. Blind-bake the crust until golden at the edges, about 20 minutes. Remove the paper and beans, and return the crust to the oven to brown all over, 10 to 15 minutes. Remove to a cooling rack.

FROM THE BREWERY, VINEYARD, AND CASK

From winemaking to beer brewing to distilling, Maine is becoming one of the best regions for adventurous drinkers to explore craft brews and spirits.

Maine's resurgent grain industry is supplying a growing number of farm-to-glass brewers and distillers with locally grown rye, wheat, barley, and oats. Winemakers in Maine have long used orchard fruits, native berries, and even rhubarb to make both sweet and dry wines, but in recent years, some wineries have started growing grapes for a small line of unique, truly local vintages. Even a forward-thinking potato farm is finding a use for potatoes that don't make the market cut, turning them into crystal clear top-shelf vodka.

While wineries, distillers, and breweries are sprouting up statewide, the largest concentration is occurring in Portland; a particular concentration of beer-, spirit-, wine-, and kombucha-tasting rooms in the once-industrial East Bayside neighborhood has inspired the nickname "Yeast Bayside."

This is all good news for entrepreneurial farmers who want to try their hand at growing hops or other unique crops used for alcohol production.

BARTLETT MAINE ESTATE WINERY AND DISTILLERY

GOULDSBORO

On an Augusta evening sometime in the early 1980s, Bob Bartlett was sipping a glass of wine at a Blaine House reception.

It was his wine, crafted from Maine-grown fruits at his fledgling winery in Gouldsboro and as identifiable to him as an infant would be to any parent. But when asked by a fellow guest which of his varieties they were sampling, he was embarrassed to admit that he could not identify it.

"I knew it was mine," Bob recounts, "but I just couldn't put my finger on which one."

"At the time, the state was trying to promote Maine agriculture," Bob explains. Bob and his wife, Kathe, had just opened their winery, and for-

mer Governor Joe Brennan invited them down to the Blaine House for a special reception where their wines would be served.

On a hunch, Bob wandered back into the kitchen and discovered that the catering staff had decanted the wine into pitchers—separated not by varietal, but by color; all the reds into one pitcher, and all the whites into another.

Bob laughed it off. "It was early days in Maine," he says.

Bob, a native of Detroit, had spent summers in midcoast Maine as a child and always wanted to come back to the state to live. By the early seventies, Bob had built a successful career as both a glass artist and an architect, but was ready for a change. After going back to school for winemaking, he and Kathe started exploring the idea of moving to Maine and starting a winery.

In 1975, the couple did just that.

"At first, we tried growing grapes," Bob says. But when that didn't work, the couple decided to try making high-quality dry fruit wines from fruits that were already growing well in Maine.

"It was a stupid business idea," Bob says, explaining that there was zero demand for fruit wine at the time nor were there other commercial wineries in Maine, plus it wasn't even legal to operate a tasting room. But the Bartletts were determined to build a life for themselves in the state they loved. So, they started experimenting with the fruit that was literally right outside their door: wild Maine blueberries.

Meanwhile, Bob began to design, and then to build, the winery and tasting room. After all, he thought, if they were going to try to make and sell fruit wines, they would first need a way of getting people to try them.

"I actually wrote the legislation that made testing rooms legal," Bob says. And when the bill became law in 1983, Bartlett Winery was ready with their first bottles.

They opened their tasting room doors that same year with 600 gallons of five different wines, made from blueberries, apples, and pears. And they sold out in two weeks. The next year, they doubled production, and every year after that. At the winery's most productive, they were making about 8,000 to 10,000 cases—or 19,000 to 24,000 gallons—annually.

As the winery's reputation has grown, and the wines keep winning awards year after year, the Bartletts have resisted pressure to industrialize and increase production. Bob says they'd rather keep it small and local, with a focus on experimentation.

These days, the winery makes about 3,000 cases of wine, and has expanded into distilling. Their distillery products include an award-winning rum made with organic molasses.

As an industry pioneer, Bob says he's humbled by the radical growth of wine-making and distilling in Maine, and notes that it's gratifying to see the amount of support there is for newcomers.

"I started with a certain amount of ignorance," Bob says. "But, we had a passion and a doggedness that is important to have in business. If we had listened to everyone else, we might not have done it."

Sangria-Style Rum

SERVES 2

Strawberry season is late in Maine compared to most strawberry-growing states, so by the time these first of the season's berries are ready to pick, most Mainers are in full summer mode. This celebratory rosy-colored drink is a great way to kick off barbecue season in the yard or Sunday brunch on the deck.

1 cup iced hibiscus tea

½ cup rum

1 tablespoon simple syrup

1 tablespoon lemon juice

1 tablespoon strawberry liqueur

1 dash Angostura or Peychaud's bitters

1 cup ice cubes

½ cup strawberries, hulled and halved

½ lemon, thinly sliced

1. Stir together the tea, rum, simple syrup, lemon juice, strawberry liqueur, bitters, and ice cubes in a cocktail shaker or bar glass until the outside of the shaker or glass is very cold, about 30 to 45 seconds.

2. Divide the strawberries and lemon slices between two serving glasses before dividing the cocktail (and ice cubes) between them.

The Rum Rusticator

SERVES 2

Rum is made from sugar cane, so although almost every Maine distiller makes it, there is no true Maine rum. However, rum has a long and motley history in the coastal ports of the state and among seafarers both modern and of old. Portland has a particular affinity for the spirit, notorious for the violent, well-fabled Rum Riot of 1855, which sprang from the discovery of Portland Mayor Neal Dow's hidden stash of alcohol during a time of extremely unpopular prohibition laws in the state.

This cocktail, made from freshly pressed apple juice, maple syrup, and dark rum, is appropriate for an outdoor cocktail party in the late summer or early fall.

3 crisp, fresh apples

½ cup dark rum

1 tablespoon lemon juice

1 tablespoon pure maple syrup

2 dashes Angostura bitters

1½ cups ice cubes

2 lemon peel twists

1. Core two apples and cut into chunks. Pass the chunks through a juicer, collecting the juice in a cocktail shaker or bar glass.

2. Add the rum, lemon juice, maple syrup, bitters, and ice cubes. Stir with a bar spoon until the outside of the shaker or bar glass is very cold.

3. Divide between two cocktail glasses, adding some of the ice cubes from the shaker or glass.

4. Cut the remaining apple into thin slices and arrange in the cocktails along with the lemon peel.

CELLARDOOR WINERY & VINEYARD

LINCOLNVILLE

Anyone who's met Bettina Doulton, the dynamic founder and owner of Cellardoor Winery, knows that she is on a mission to not only produce excellent wine from well-cultivated Maine-grown grapes, but to also have a good time doing it. Don't think it's possible to grow quality wine grapes in Maine? Try telling her that. Bettina, a cancer survivor who dramatically shifted career paths after her illness went into remission, is used to doing the impossible.

Cellardoor's close-knit team make wines from a vineyard they planted together in 2008 on 5 acres of gently cascading fertile valley in mid-coast Maine. The vineyard's 5,000 vines include four varieties of high-quality, cold-hardy grapes: Marquette, Frontenac Blanc, Frontenac Gris, and L'Acadie Blanc.

Their first harvest in 2012 totaled four and a half tons of grapes, which were blended to produce their first estate wine, the award-winning sparkling rosé Vendange. In 2013, they harvested enough grapes to produce two estate wines—a sparkling rosé and sparkling white.

The winery also produces award-winning wines from other domestic grapes, and operates a tasting room, retail store, and event space in a 200-year-old barn on the vineyard property.

Rhubarb Frosé

SERVES 4

Eighteen Twenty Wines, located in the East Bayside neighborhood of Portland, specializes in making wines from easy-to-grow, complex-tasting rhubarb. Winemaker Amanda O'Brien likes to say that rhubarb wine is the new rosé, and this recipe celebrates the similarity.

750 milliliters dry rhubarb wine (or rosé,
if you can't find rhubarb wine)

½ cup granulated sugar

½ cup water

1⅔ cups hulled and halved strawberries

4 tablespoons fresh lemon juice

1 cup crushed ice

1. Pour rosé into a 13-by-9-inch cake pan. Freeze until almost solid, about 6 hours.

2. Combine the sugar with the water in a heavy-bottomed saucepan. Bring to a boil over moderate heat, stirring until sugar has dissolved.

3. Remove the saucepan from the heat and add the strawberries. Let sit for 30 minutes to infuse.

4. Strain the syrup through a fine sieve into a small bowl. Cover and chill.

5. Once the rosé is almost frozen solid, scrape into a blender and add the lemon juice, ½ cup strawberry syrup, and crushed ice.

6. Blend on high until pureed. Transfer to a freezer-proof container, cover, and freeze for 30 minutes.

7. Scrape semi-frozen rosé into blender and pulse again until slushy. Divide between glasses.

ALLAGASH BREWERY

PORTLAND

In 1995, when Rob Tod released his first batch of beer from the humble digs of his newly founded brewery in an industrial park in Portland, no one wanted to drink it.

His flagship beer, a Belgian-style wheat beer brewed with coriander and orange peel, looked and tasted different than the crystal-clear lagers the local population was used to. But with some innovative packaging (four-packs!), and a cascade of gold medals from national competitions, Rob managed to get the beer in the people's hands, and the people found that they liked it.

The company still brews beer from the exact spot where Rob started with his hand-welded brewing system, but the company has become one of Maine's business icons, inspiring dogged entrepreneurship and a groundswell of local breweries to lay down roots in Maine. Their state-of-the-art brewery on Industrial Way has attracted distillers, food producers, and other breweries to set up facilities in the area, creating a bustling beer and spirit "village" in an otherwise less-trafficked part of Portland.

While Allagash has been utilizing Maine-grown grains, hops, and fruits to brew their beers from the get-go, in 2017, Rob took that commitment a step further and pledged that by 2021, his brewery would be using one million pounds of Maine-grown grain per year.

Since 1995, Allagash earned its B Corp certification, Rob Tod has received a James Beard Award, and he, his team, and their beer have been recognized all over the world for modern innovation, adherence to tradition, and general excellence.

MAINE DISTILLERIES

FREEPORT

In 2005, Don and Lee Thibodeau, a couple of potato farming brothers, launched an idea they hoped would make their off-grade potatoes profitable: They would make vodka with them.

Maine Distilleries's Cold River Vodka is made with potatoes from Don's Green Thumb Farm in western Maine. The hand-crafted vodka is perhaps the only family-owned "ground-to-glass" vodka operation in the world.

The company also produces Cold River Blueberry Vodka, made with Maine blueberries, Cold River Gin, and a golden-colored Distiller's Reserve Vodka, which has been aged in oak barrels for two years.

Cider Shandy

SERVES 2

Serve this nontraditional shandy on a hot summer or early fall afternoon in large frosty glasses. Since both the soda and the beer are carbonated, you can choose either a still or effervescent cider, depending on how much you like bubbles.

½ cup sparkling lemonade or lemon-lime soda, chilled

½ cup hard apple cider, chilled

1 small lemon, cut into thin slices

1 crisp, fresh apple, cored and thinly sliced

Two 12-ounce bottles lager or pilsner, chilled

1. Divide the lemonade (or lemon-lime soda), cider, lemon, and apple slices between two chilled pint glasses.

2. Top up with the beer and serve straight away.

PORTERSFIELD CIDER

POWNAL

Located on his southern Maine farm, David Buchanan's small-batch cidery and tasting room bottles and serves dry, lightly conditioned ciders. The ciders are made from wild apples foraged from all over Maine as well as heritage varieties from his own orchards.

David travels the back roads of Maine in search of abandoned trees, grafting the best of them to raise on his farm. His ciders are slowly fermented and his goal is to coax and showcase the wide range of flavors the apples can produce. The finished ciders, much like wine, are blended to pair with food.

The farm makes only 2,000 gallons of cider annually, and most are available only at the Portersfield Cider tasting room.

NEW ENGLAND DISTILLING

PORTLAND

Ned Wight comes from a long line of Maryland distillers. But the New England Distilling owner built his own company from scratch, making unique ultra-small batch spirits in a copper still in a small, industrial warehouse in Portland.

Ned's passion for home-beer brewing eventually landed him a job at Allagash Brewery, and, given his family history, distilling seemed like the natural progression. Ned set out on his own as New England Distilling in 2011.

Most of his spirits are produced with Maine-grown grain, and his product line has grown to five unique, hand-bottled spirits, including gin, rye, bourbon, rum, and a special whiskey distilled from Allagash Brewery's Saison Ale.

Maine Maple Old Fashioned

SERVES 2

This unusually spiced cocktail is suitable for a winter cocktail party. The addition of strong spices and maple syrup play equal parts in tempering the burn of the alcohol while also warming you from the inside out.

4 ounces bourbon

2 whole star anise pods

4 cardamom pods, lightly crushed

2 teaspoons maple syrup

2 dashes Angostura bitters

Ice cubes

1. Stir together bourbon, star anise, and cardamom in a small glass. Cover and let stand for 1 hour.

2. Fine-strain infused whiskey into an old-fashioned glass and add maple syrup and bitters, stirring until syrup has dissolved.

3. Add ice cubes and garnish with the star anise used in step 1.

FROM THE PANTRY

Preserving and canning the season's surplus harvests is a long-standing cottage industry in Maine. Almost every family has a time-honored recipe for zucchini relish, strawberry jam, or dill pickles. Stovetop water-bath canners are a popular commodity in home cellars and are pressed into service each summer as gardeners try to keep up with avalanching harvests.

Lacto-fermented vegetables, such as sauerkraut and pickles, are rising in popularity due to their many health benefits. In turn, they are becoming an important value-added product from farms cutting down on the diversity of their vegetable crops in an effort to decrease field time and increase profitability.

Elderberry Jelly

MAKES ROUGHLY 7 HALF-PINT JARS

Not just for toast, elderberry jelly is a fantastic addition to rich meat stews, or used to liven up a humdrum barbecue sauce. A softened elderberry jelly is a gorgeous glaze for a traditional cheesecake, but I especially love it with a softly spiced pumpkin cheesecake in lieu of the traditional Thanksgiving pumpkin pie.

4 pounds fresh elderberries

½ cup water

Granulated sugar, according to direction in step 3

Juice of 2 lemons

1. Put the elderberries into a large heavy-bottomed saucepan. Crush well to release their juice, then add the water. Bring to a boil, cover, and simmer for about 15 minutes, or until tender.

2. Ladle the fruit and juices into a sterilized jelly bag. Strain the juice through the jelly bag overnight into a bowl. Do not squeeze the bag or the jelly will be cloudy.

3. Measure the juice into a large heavy-bottomed pan and, to every 20 fluid ounces of juice, add 1 pound of sugar. Stir in the lemon juice.

4. Heat the juice and sugar in the pan and stir over a low heat until the sugar has dissolved completely. Bring to a boil and cook until the mixture reaches 220°F.

5. Pour the jelly immediately into just-sterilized jars. Cover and seal immediately, and invert the jars for 5 minutes.

Sweetcorn Relish

MAKES ROUGHLY 8 FOUR-OUNCE JARS

Sweet and spicy relishes of all kinds fill the stalls at the fall farmers' markets, as farmers find ways to use surplus produce, as well as add value to their fresh goods.

4 cobs sweetcorn

1 red bell pepper, seeds removed and diced

1 green bell pepper, seeds removed and diced

1 stalk celery, thinly sliced

1 small red chile, seeds removed and chopped (optional)

1 onion, peeled and chopped

2 cups white wine vinegar

1 cup granulated sugar

2 teaspoons salt

2 teaspoons mustard powder

½ teaspoon ground turmeric

1. Strip the kernels from the cobs with a sharp knife. Scrape them into a pan of boiling water and cook for 2 minutes. Drain well.

2. Put the sweetcorn kernels and the remaining ingredients into a large saucepan. Heat gently, stirring until the sugar has dissolved, then bring to a boil, stirring frequently, and cook for 15 to 20 minutes until slightly thickened. It should be a spoonable consistency, but not as thick as chutney.

3. Pour the relish immediately into just-sterilized jars. Immediately cover, seal, and invert the jars for 5 minutes.

NERVOUS NELLIE'S

DEER ISLE

On a twisting island backroad on the remote, rocky outpost of Deer Isle, artist Peter Beerits and his wife, Anne, have been producing jams, jellies, and chutneys made from Maine fruit since 1984. The small-batch company produces 50,000 jars of 15 different kinds of preserves annually, using seven tons of fruit for the Maine Wild Blueberry jam alone.

If Peter isn't overseeing jelly production, you'll find him creating installations for the ever-expanding on-site sculpture garden he calls Nellieville. The whimsical roadside attraction features movie-like sets populated with the artist's life-sized characters sculpted out of found materials.

Nellie is among one of Peter's fantastical characters. She is a red, birdlike creature who not only makes an appearance on the labels of his jams and chutneys, but is also the protagonist in a series of graphic novels that chronicle Nellie's journey "in search of the place, far off on the edge of things, where the sun springs fresh and new out of the morning sea." There are currently eight volumes in the series.

Anne and Peter's preserves can be found in grocery stores statewide, but loyal customers and curious visitors can also visit the homestead year-round, where they can tour the grounds, shop for locally made crafts in the Nervous Nellie's gift shop, or enjoy a cup of coffee and a pastry in the attached cafe.

Rhubarb Chutney

MAKES ROUGHLY 8 FOUR-OUNCE JARS

There's nothing better than rhubarb chutney on a roast loin of local pork or venison. Tart, sweet, and savory all at once, it's as essential as mint with lamb. For the best color (and to keep the chutney descending in muddy hues) use thin-stalked ruby-red rhubarb, which holds its color all the way through its fibrous center.

2 cups apple cider vinegar

2¼ cups granulated sugar

2 teaspoon salt

3 large onions, roughly chopped

6 cloves garlic, peeled

1¾ ounces fresh peeled and finely chopped ginger

2 pounds rhubarb, cut into chunks

1. Place the vinegar, sugar, salt, onions, garlic cloves, and ginger in a large pan and slowly bring to a boil, stirring from time to time.

2. Turn up the heat and boil rapidly for 5 minutes.

3. Add the rhubarb and continue cooking for 15 minutes, stirring from time to time to prevent the chutney from burning.

4. Pour the hot chutney immediately into the recently sterilized jars, cover, seal, and invert for 5 minutes.

THIRTY ACRE FARM

WHITEFIELD

In 2004, Simon and Jane Frost started growing vegetables on land that hadn't been farmed in 40 years. At the time, they had no practical experience with farming, but they had a passion for preserving the very best organic vegetables with lacto-fermentation—a process that utilizes the natural yeasts in fresh produce to create a living brine. Lacto-fermentation is an effective way to preserve harvests and turn them into a healthy, tasty condiment.

Today, Thirty Acre Farm produces a dozen or more varieties of kraut, kimchi, pickles, and hot sauces, and they grow roughly 95 percent of what they ferment. They currently harvest over 100,000 pounds of organic produce each year, and their fermented products are distributed throughout Maine, Massachusetts, and New Hampshire.

Red Onion and Jalapeño Quick Pickle

MAKES 1 QUART JAR

El El Frijoles's chef Michele Levesque makes this quick pickle for the restaurant's Lobster Tacos (page 174). This recipe makes much more than you need for the tacos, but Michele says the pickle will keep in the refrigerator for two weeks. That is, of course, if you don't use it up by putting it on everything from sandwiches to scrambled eggs.

2½ large red onions, thinly sliced

2 jalapeños, thinly sliced (Michele will leave the seeds in for an extra kick)

1 cup water

1 cup rice wine vinegar

2 tablespoons sea salt

2 tablespoons granulated sugar

1. Place all ingredients into a medium saucepan and give them a stir.

2. Bring the mixture up to a boil over a medium-high flame.

3. As soon as the mixture boils, immediately remove the pan from the heat and allow to cool.

4. Transfer to a canning jar or other container with an airtight lid and store in your refrigerator.

MORSE'S SAUERKRAUT

WALDOBORO

More than 100 years ago on his family farm in Waldoboro, Virgil Morse started making naturally fermented sauerkraut from an old German recipe passed down to him from relatives in the old country. By 1918, he had turned kraut-making into a commercial enterprise and it remained the family business for close to 80 years.

Since 1991, the business has evolved into a German restaurant and extensive European deli, and has changed hands three times. Today, owners Cody Lamontagne and James Gammon operate it out of the same building Virgil and his son built to house the operation in 1947. And at the heart of it all is the exact same recipe for sauerkraut Virgil started making more than a century ago.

The kraut, made with cabbage from neighboring White Oak Farm is naturally fermented (a process called lacto-fermentation) by weighing down freshly shredded cabbage mixed with salt. The cabbage ferments in its own juice and becomes a living thing full of natural yeasts and probiotics. It is widely available in the refrigerated section of grocery stores all over Maine, but getting the kraut from the source has become a pilgrimage for fresh kraut lovers from all over.

Morse's is open year-round, and most people need a good map to find it. But all of them seem to agree that it's worth the trip.

Lacto-Fermented Sauerkraut

MAKES 1 QUART JAR

Making fresh sauerkraut is more about the process than the recipe, but below is a guide to getting you started if you're inspired to try it. Once you get familiar with the process of lacto-fermentation, you'll want to try it with all sorts of vegetables.

1 head green or red cabbage

1 to 2 tablespoons sea salt

1. Quarter, core, and thinly slice the cabbage. If you have one, a mandolin makes quick work of this. Reserve a large leaf.

2. Place the sliced cabbage in a large bowl and sprinkle in the salt.

3. With clean hands, massage the salt into the cabbage. Eventually, the cabbage will soften and release its juice. This might take 5 to 10 minutes. You don't need to massage the cabbage the entire time.

4. Pack the cabbage into a ½-gallon canning jar. You will need to press the cabbage down with your fist every so often so that you can fit it all into the jar. Pour any liquid from the bowl into the jar. The cabbage should be completely submerged in the liquid.

5. Place the reserved cabbage leaf over the surface of the shredded cabbage. Then place a clean rock (or a smaller canning jar full of rocks) on top of the leaf so that the shredded cabbage is completely submerged.

6. Secure a clean cloth over the top of the jar with a rubber band, and set the jar away from direct sunlight.

7. Let the kraut ferment for 3 days at a cool room temperature. Check it often and press down on it so that the shredded cabbage remains submerged at all times.

8. After 3 days, taste the kraut. If it's pleasantly sour and tangy enough to suit your taste, cap the jar and store it in the refrigerator; it is ready to eat. Otherwise, continue to ferment at room temperature until the kraut suits your taste.

THE MAINE MENU

JANUARY: COZY DINNER WITH FRIENDS
Brown Bread and Misty Brook Farm's
   Home Churned Butter
Potato and Mustard Gratin
Blue Hill Blondes Oven-Baked Short Ribs
Snell Farm Apple Pie

FEBRUARY: APRES SKI BRUNCH
Cranberry-Orange Scones with Citrus Glaze
Elderberry Blinis with Caramelized Apples
Meg Mitchell's Sweet Onion Pie
Potato Wedges with Rosemary
Raspberry Trifle

MARCH: CABIN FEVER RELIEVER COCKTAIL PARTY
Crostini with Chicken Liver and
   Caramelized Shallots
Oysters au Gratin
Sautéed Wild Mushrooms with Thyme
Honey Butter Popcorn
Rum Rusticator
Baked Mini Apple Cider Donuts
Blueberry Ginger Cake

APRIL: MAPLE CELEBRATION
Maple Old Fashioned
Maple Baked Beans
Pan-Baked Corn Bread
Ployes with vanilla ice cream and maple syrup

MAY: CINCO DE MAYO, MAINE STYLE
Tortillería Pachanga Chorizo Molotes
Rhubarb Frosé
El El Frijoles Lobster Tacos
Panna Cotta with Raspberries

JUNE: MAINE SPRING SUPPER
Beet and Arugula Bruschetta with
   Chive Goat Cheese Spread
Mushroom Soup with Chanterelles

Pan-Roasted Lamb Chops with Mint
   Pesto and Carrot Puree
Spinach with Toasted Garlic
Rhubarb Tart with Strawberries,
   Mascarpone, and Rhubarb Coulis

JULY: DOORYARD BARBECUE
Grilled Tomatoes with Herbs on Garlic Toast
Chicken Wings with Blueberry Barbecue Sauce
Grilled Halibut with Spiced Butter Sauce
Creme Anglaise with Grilled Nectarines
   or Peaches

AUGUST: MID-SUMMER SEAFOOD FEAST
Oysters on the Half Shell with
   Shallot Mignonette
Fried Clams
Steamed Maine Lobster
Potato Wedges with Rosemary
Two Fat Cats Lemon-Zucchini Whoopie
   Pies with Blueberry Filling
Blueberry Tart

SEPTEMBER: LATE SUMMER SUPPER
Classic Crab Cakes
Erin French's Fried Green Tomatoes
   with Buttermilk & Chives
Sara Jenkins's Eggplant Parmesan
Apple and Blackberry Crumble

OCTOBER: "GAME" NIGHT
Sautéed Wild Mushrooms with Thyme
Buttermilk Biscuits
Moose Bourguignon
Wild Fern Apple-Cranberry Pie

NOVEMBER: A NEW ENGLAND THANKSGIVING
Crostini with Chicken Liver and
   Caramelized Shallots
Corn Soup with Parsley

Pan-Roasted Duck Breast with
  Chestnuts and Brussels Sprouts
Creamed Pearl Onons
Roasted Acorn Squash with Brown Sugar and Butter
Young Carrots with Lemon, Thyme, and Olive Oil
Cornmeal Pudding
Baked Apples with Cider Sauce

DECEMBER: THE HOLIDAY TABLE
Oysters with Cucumber Sauce
Individual Pork Pies with Cranberries
Cream of Lobster Soup
Filet Mignon with Peppered Pears
Spinach with Toasted Garlic
Blackberry and Almond Torte

INDEX

*Italics are used to show illustrations.